FAI
FOR A
GLAD FOOL

Wilfred Wood

FAITH
FOR A
GLAD FOOL

The Church of England's
First Black Bishop speaks on
Racial Justice, Christian
Faith, Love and Sacrifice

WILFRED WOOD

With foreword by the Rt Rev'd Colin Buchanan

 New Beacon Books

First published 2010 by New Beacon Books Ltd., 76 Stroud Green Road, London N4 3EN
Reprinted 2010

© 2010 Wilfred Wood

'Life Experience With Britannia' reprinted from *Building Britannia* by kind permission of New Beacon Books Ltd.

ISBN 978 1 873201 23 0

Front cover: On the steps of St Paul's Cathedral following the consecration service, 25th July 1985
From left to right: Bishop Colin Buchanan, the Most Reverend Robert Runcie, then Archbishop of Canterbury, Bishop Wilfred Wood, Rev'd John Witheridge.
Back cover: The 'precious mitre' pictured was made by the nuns of the Community of St Peter at Woking in Surrey, and is over a hundred years old. It was a consecration gift. With my retirement I passed it on to the Archbishop of York who in due course will pass it on to a bishop after him.

Printed by Imprint Digital, Exeter, England

Dedication

To God, in thanksgiving for my parents, my wife Ina,
our five children and their four spouses, our seven
grandchildren, my other relatives and friends, and the
many colleagues, ordained and lay, particularly in
Shepherd's Bush, Catford, and Southwark diocese,
and the Rev'd Sandra Hazell and the congregation of
St Lawrence Church, Barbados, all of whom in various
ways have held me up as I stumbled along the
Christian journey.

I Corinthians, chapter 4 verse 10

We are fools for Christ's sake ...

FOREWORD
by Bishop Colin Buchanan

On 25 July 1985 I was privileged to have guaranteed a place in one of the most formative moments of the modern Church of England. I had been invited by Hugh Montefiore to become Bishop of Aston, that is, to be his suffragan bishop in the diocese of Birmingham. The invitation came at the end of March, and I was under pressure to respond quickly – and not only because of the pace at which Hugh Montefiore always lived, but also because in this particular case, if the announcement were long delayed, we would miss the date reserved in Archbishop Robert Runcie's diary, and would have to wait until November. But when I said 'yes' on Easter Day 1985, I had no idea with whom I might be bracketed in this procedure. In the Province of Canterbury, bishops are usually done two at a time, and it is sheer chance what particular pairing may occur on any one date; and I doubt whether I gave even passing thought to the matter, for a vast reorganisation of my own life had now to be planned and implemented against the clock, and that was all-consuming. Nevertheless, there was likely to be someone else joining with me.

In the event, my companion consecrand was named publicly before I was – and he was named midst a blaze of lights and publicity. It was one Wilfred Wood, the Archdeacon of Southwark, and he was becoming a suffragan within the same diocese of Southwark – nominated by Ronald Bowlby, he was to be Bishop of Croydon. I had never met him, though I had seen him at a distance once or twice, but, of course, I knew immediately who he was and what this implied. For

Wilfred was BLACK. And I had picked the longest of long straws (no doubt, all within the economy of God) as to who my fellow-consecrand should be. And, as this publication is scheduled to mark the twenty-fifth anniversary of our shared consecration, I hope I may be forgiven for lingering a little on that event.

I got in touch with Wilfred quickly and introduced myself, and he was very gracious about how we should each contribute to the service in St Paul's. Despite my saying above that I saw the significance of his becoming a bishop, with hindsight I can see that I was actually insufficiently aware. Bishops and archbishops were coming from round the world to lay a hand on this astonishing entrant into the Church of England's episcopate.[1] Thousands and thousands of black Christians were rejoicing at his nomination. The diocese of Southwark lay yards away from St Paul's across the Thames, and they would fill St Paul's. Because Wilfred Wood was being made bishop, this was an event of awe and wonder. It was writing history. And I was to share it with him. My own shorthand description of it since the day has been to say that I had a small walk-on part in a great Caribbean event. And the service was videoed, and the video went twice round the world and seventeen times round the Caribbean, and I have fondly imagined to myself audiences everywhere saying in a casual moment 'I wonder who that pale fellow beside him is, or where he was going to?'

Wilfred and I presented a great contrast. I was white, from a minor public-school and Oxbridge, principal of a Theological College which at that point had never even had a black Church of England ordinand. I was at least a semi-academic, and had never been an incumbent. And I was an unreconstructed evangelical with more than a touch of the puritan about me, and so I came from a constituency with a long-inherited suspicion of bishops, and even a marginal embarrassment at joining their ranks. Wilfred by contrast came from the colourful but relaxed catholicism of the West Indies; he had been at Codrington College (being tutored by the Mirfield Fathers) in Barbados twenty-five years before; and he had ministered at street-level amongst disadvantaged people of varied ethnicities in relatively deprived areas of England for most of those twenty-five years. Furthermore, he had no embarrassment about episcopacy whatsoever – from the best possible motives and in the best possible way he was going to revel in it. To utilize a metaphor I have heard Wilfred himself use, but he would forbid to me, the contrast between us was truly a black-and-white one. And the contrast was further sharply etched by the paradox that Wilfred was going to the Croydon Area of Southwark diocese – that is, the area of the Surrey stockbroker belt, the diocesan white highlands – while I was going to the city of Birmingham, in fact to live in Handsworth, in what was arguably the most intensely multi-ethnic city of Western Europe. I came from Croydon and knew something of it, and I said to Wilfred 'It's Birmingham that needs a black bishop, not Croydon', and to this he helpfully replied 'Well, come on, man, don't be lacking in ambition – perhaps one day you can be a black bishop'.

The very comedy of suggesting I might change my colour was also part of the irony – and scandal – of the situation. A particular unchangeable feature of our common humanity had been that which had labelled his ancestors as fit for sale and transportation as slaves; and that same unchangeable feature was encountering resentment and discrimination in twentieth century Britain. Nor were the Churches wholly free from this attitude; the standardized report said that sidesmen on Anglican church doors would say (perhaps quite kindly) to black Christians coming there for the first time 'Oh, your church is down the next street', and direct them to a 'black pentecostalist' assembly. I have met African-Caribbean folk who had themselves met this treatment; and I have known enough of the black-majority churches in Britain to have seen the results. Yet Anglicanism has had a great history in the West Indies and many many of those who migrated to England from the days of the *Empire Windrush* in 1948 onwards had never thought of themselves as other than Anglicans.

Meeting Wilfred for the first time as we were becoming bishops, I only slowly got his past career into focus. He was a Barbadian who had been ordained deacon when finishing at Codrington in 1961, but was answering a call for Black Anglican clergy to minister in the areas of immigration in the diocese of London, and came over in August 1962 in his diaconate, and was ordained presbyter soon after. He pioneered the role to which he was called, taking assistants' posts in parishes initially, but from 1967 also serving as the Bishop of London's chaplain for community relations – a role which gave him ample opportunity both to identify with a great swathe of new Commonwealth citizens in London, and also to take up cudgels at intervals on their behalf. At each stage he must have had a lonely path to pursue – there were few, if any, role-models; there were also grieving families not wanting a black man to officiate at grandad's funeral; there was fear for both Wilfred and Ina lest their children be hounded for their colour; there were the unconcealed provocations of Enoch Powell and other senior politicians;[2] and a more widespread poisonous miasma of a large number of the English hoping out loud that all these people would some day soon 'go home'.

In 1974 David Sheppard invited him to cross the Thames and come to St Laurence, Catford, in the borough of Lewisham. Here he came ever more to public notice, pastoring a multi-ethnic congregation, becoming rural dean of East Lewisham, and raising a banner for justice in all sorts of areas. He used to love telling of the days when he annually on Christmas Day picketed South Africa House to protest against the enormities of the apartheid regime, adding in his inimitable style that, since the transition of power in South Africa, he had been deprived of a cause for protest and was left twiddling his thumbs on Christmas Day. Back in Lewisham, I was myself to pick up sixteen years later the impact he had made in rallying to the support of the families (all black) who had lost teenage children in the infamous New Cross Fire in 1981. It was not only not surprising – it was obviously simply sensible that Wilfred was invited to join the Archbishop's Commission on Urban Priority Areas, and was a party, with three others from ethnic minorities, to its far-reaching recommendations in their report, *Faith in the City* (Church House Publishing, December 1985). I well recall him reflecting later on those three years of going round the country, staying in insalubrious places and encountering needy and disadvantaged people; for he made the simple but profound remark: 'The thing I remember most vividly is the smells – I rarely get them now'!

Faith in the City was published less than five months after our consecration, and so by then I knew the man and could see his hand in it. One particular strand relating to racial discrimination was the proposal for the Church of England to establish a Central Commission for racial justice. Synod declined to do this, but after some hiccups did establish a Committee for Black Anglican Concerns, with Wilfred himself, having been elected to the House of Bishops by his fellow suffragans, as the chairman and convenor.[3] Synodical rebuffs were not over – the CBAC came to Synod with a proposal that there should be reserved places for Black Anglicans within the Houses of Clergy and Laity; this was rejected, and, although I think it was electorally self-defeating and synodically a very bad precedent, it was only too easy to read the defeat as a simple racist slap in the face exercised by the sitting members against an unwanted minority. Wilfred ran his time as chair of CBAC, and was followed in the role by a young Ugandan presbyter, John Sentamu by name, and Wilfred himself became a kind of episcopal guardian of it. Our paths were crossing again, as, when I was elected to the House of Bishops in 1990, I was appointed to the Council for Christian Unity, and the CCU deputed me to be their representative on the CBAC. Thus I had an [unprominent] part in the Black Anglican Celebration at York in July 1994, the occasion for one of Wilfred's notable and characteristic sermons, reprinted here on page 38.[4]

In my own life, I had forfeited my tenure as Bishop of Aston and gone into semi-exile in Kent in 1989. Wilfred was unfailingly supportive, and, as we were now near-neighbours, he secured for me a visiting role as an honorary assistant bishop in Southwark diocese. In due course the wheel turned full circle, and in late 1996 I was appointed by Bishop Roy Williamson to be Bishop of Woolwich, and thus, to my great joy, to share with Wilfred as a colleague in the Southwark episcopal team. So we ran in partnership together for the last five years of his time as a working bishop, and I was picking up his trail from his years as a vicar in Catford, followed by his three years as Archdeacon of Southwark, but sharing with him in the battles of the present time, not least in that which had so identified his ministry, seeking a just place and an emergent leadership for the ethnic minorities in the diocese of Southwark, and in the Church of England and the nation of England generally. The glare of publicity has inevitably picked Wilfred out as black, and as a pioneer and trailblazer for black people in England. In 2004 he came joint second after Mary Seacole (a volunteer nurse in the Crimean War) in the poll for the leading 100 Great Black Britons. But it would be unfair to list him as simply a single-issue man. The award of a knighthood, three honorary doctorates and the Freedom of the Borough of Croydon attest to a recognition of his wider contribution. He would never have been a bishop without a record as a man of God, a pastor, preacher and prophet. And so it is that this collection of his sermons and addresses cover a great number of occasions on which, in faithfulness to his God and to his calling, he has spoken at some depth, no little eloquence, and a great thrust of purpose to mark the occasion or to move a situation forward. The occasions are listed and they speak for themselves. Wilfred has written books before [and *Keep the Faith, Baby!* is still in print], and they share with this collection in revealing his penetration of subject matter, his ready humour, and his passionate concerns.

I should add a couple of personal notes. The first is this, that I think that I have only heard about three of Wilfred's sermons published here [bishops rarely have opportunity to hear each other – and it has only been opportunity which I have lacked], but the one that sticks most strongly in my mind was his tribute to David Sheppard in Southwark cathedral in March 2005. But that address in Southwark draws out many qualities of this man:

> Firstly, like any true West Indian, he has cricket in

his bones, and a reluctant but genuine admiration of a great English batsman – and has never hesitated to include partisan remarks about West Indies cricket in his sermons.[5]

Secondly, as one who had been appointed by David Sheppard and had hunted with him on the Archbishop's Commission on Urban Priority Areas, he reveals a tremendous respect for a privileged white Englishman who ran ahead of him in age yet sought in turn to learn from him.

Thirdly, there is an amazing underlying theme in that address [and in many after it] which you cannot learn from the text. Wilfred took retirement in 2002 with poor health. But soon after, all this was overtaken by his going blind, and everything which he has said in public since has been without the benefit of reading or writing. I cross-questioned him about this one address which I heard, and he had composed it, dictated it to Ina, had her read it back to him as many times as were necessary to learn it, and had preached it verbatim from memory. And thus there is the part of Ina to note – wholly typical of her unswerving support over nearly fifty years [and one wonders whether, living so close to his addresses and sermons, she did not make suggestions about their content?]. But there is above all a man who, at the age of sixty-six, gives himself to overcoming an enormous obstacle – one which all but the most dauntless would find incapacitating and disheartening – in order to go on ministering for the Lord whose servant he has been over so many years. [In fairness I have to add that he is now able to use a computer which identifies letters and numbers by sound, and that provision has matched and rewarded his courage – and I have little hope, as I might have had a year or two ago, that this essay can be sneaked past him into print without his ever scrutinizing it...]

So, I come to my other closing personal point. Yes, my companion in July 1985 was a blind-date. He has often referred to me as his episcopal twin. I walk tall when I hear that. He and Ina go back and forth from Barbados, where they have recovered their roots, to England where they have embedded their five children and a great tribe of grandchildren [seven and a half at the latest and clearly still counting] in the society which they have themselves helped to shape. Wilfred, my physically blind but wholly sightful twin, I have been greatly privileged to have had that walk-on part those twenty-five years ago. From my heart in the name of our risen Lord, I salute you.

Notes

1. Comically enough, the lower echelon decision-takers at St Paul's cathedral had concluded from long experience that 40 – 50 bishops attempting to lay a hand on two candidates became an unseemly rugby scrum, visually untidy and ritually uncontrollable, and so decreed that it would be more edifying to have the assisting bishops stand around in dignified support, while simply the presenting bishops with the epistoller and gospeller actually laid on a hand. The two candidates were horrified at this antiseptic welcome for their friends, and, being entertained at Lambeth Palace overnight, raised the matter with the chief consecrator. He gave instant assurance on the point; and so Wilfred and I got word into the changing-rooms the next day – in my case, saying to Leslie Brown, who was blind and had come from Cambridge with some difficulty, 'Take no notice of anyone saying you shouldn't lay on a hand – use your elbows to get there, and do make sure you lay a hand on me'. Wilfred no doubt instructed his supporters' club more forcefully than that...
2. One such was the famous Smethwick by-election in autumn

1964, when a Labour stronghold was turned around to elect a Tory, some of whose supporters had campaigned under the banner of 'If you want a nigger for your neighbour, vote Labour'!

3. I had some interest in this by-election, as I too was a candidate (I had been a founder-member of General Synod and had served 15 years there prior to becoming a bishop). In the General Election of 1985 I had run for election by the Canterbury suffragan bishops, who had six seats, and I had mustered minimal support. When this by-election came to fill a single vacancy in 1987, I was very torn and I put in my electoral address then, as again in 1990, that, although I was keen to be elected, I thought that voters should put Wilfred above me in their preferential voting (the point being that the Church of England uses the fairest form of voting, the Single Transferable Vote in multi-member constituencies). In 1987 he filled the one casual vacancy; in 1990, with six vacancies, he was elected before me, and I just scraped in as no. 6.

4. A fuller view of the CBAC, including the York Celebration, is in my own book, *Taking the Long View: Three and a Half Decades of General Synod* (Church House Publishing, 2006) chapter 10. A fuller view still is in Glynne Gordon-Carter's account, *An Amazing Journey*.

5. I haven't asked him this, but I suspect he is of a generation that produced the famous trio of Worrell, Weekes and Walcott, and one can see how a Wood fits with them. It must be a comfort to remember the great men sometimes today.

PREFACE

'It has taken the Church nineteen hundred and eighty five years to do this, and I am not going to miss it!' This was the characteristically robust declaration from Lloyd Ethelbert 'Boy-Child' Smith CBE, the colourful Barbadian parliamentarian and my wife's father, when there developed a hitch in departure times of the flights from Barbados to the UK. The event he was referring to was the service in St Paul's Cathedral, London, on 25th July, 1985, at which I was consecrated Bishop of Croydon in the diocese of Southwark, thus becoming the first black bishop in the history of the Church of England. I was privileged to share this occasion with the highly respected Principal of St John's Theological College, Nottingham, the Rev'd Colin Buchanan, Biblical scholar, author and theologian, who was consecrated Bishop of Aston in the diocese of Birmingham. So began another of the many blessings of my life – our twenty-five years [to date] of faithful friendship.

This publication is to mark my twenty-five years as a bishop in the Church of God, in thanksgiving for the goodness, generosity and graciousness of God in His dealings with me. Included in this is His providence of many persons whose prayers, support, love, loyalty and sometimes sacrifice have contributed to whatever good I may have managed to do. They are too numerous to mention all by name, and I hope others will understand and forgive, that going back only as far as my arrival in the UK I name only the late Canon Roderick Gibbs and his wife Joan, Prebendary John Asbridge and his wife Jennifer (former Vicars of St Stephen with St Thomas, Shepherd's Bush) John D. H.

Downing (fellow curate), a friend from whom, to this day, I continue to learn much, John and Dorothy Ramsay, Wally Hayes, the Rev'd John Shand, the Rt Rev'd E. J. K. Roberts, the Rt Rev'd David Sheppard, and last but not least, the Rt Rev'd Ronnie Bowlby, the wise and thoughtful man of prayer who nominated me for appointment and guided me in my early years in the Episcopate.

One of the many blessings ordained ministry confers is the number of wonderful people it brings into one's life. Some of these may be household names, but the vast majority may, as Thomas Gray noted in his 'Elegy Written in a Country Churchyard' be 'village Hampdens, mute Miltons and guiltless Cromwells' who witnessed to Christ to the best of their ability in their corner of God's world. It fell to me to preach at the funerals of many such ordinary Christians, and the inclusion of some of these addresses is an inadequate tribute to them. May they rest in Christ and be raised with Him in glory.

I take this opportunity to record my thanks to a number of people who have helped to make this publication possible. To Sarah White and publishers 'New Beacon Books' who certainly do not anticipate a howling commercial success, and who have also kindly allowed me to include my George Padmore lecture from their publication *Building Britannia*. To my daughter Gillian Wood for her assistance in editing, and my daughter-in-law Fiona Wood for her assistance with design, and to Derek Maddicks who took the photographs on the cover, to my friend Aaron 'Buddy' Larrier and my son David Wood who ensured the safe conveyance of the manuscript from Barbados to the publishers. I would also like to thank Linda Treacy for her efforts in converting some of my older work into a more user friendly format!

And finally to my 'episcopal twin' Colin Buchanan for his generous Foreword. To these must be added the long suffering ladies who typed the addresses in the first place, namely my wife Ina, and secretaries Joyce Lechmere, Cynthia Timms, Doreen Husbands and Sylvia Pepperell. They were often the uncomplaining victims of my compulsive need to fill even the tiniest space with writing! I thank God for them all.

+Wilfred D. Wood
Barbados, February 2010

CONTENTS

SECTION TWO: CALLED TO SERVE

SECTION ONE
TOWARDS RACIAL JUSTICE

Bishop Wilfred Wood on the day of his consecration, 25 July 1985, shown here with, from left tor right:
Martin Luther King III, Wilfred Wood, and Dick Gregory

1

In the Fullness of Time: President Barack Obama's election

St Lawrence Church, Barbados, 9 November 2008

St John, chapter 14 verse 1 Jesus said:
Let not your heart be troubled:
ye believe in God, believe also in me.

*Like everyone else, I would love to live a long life –
longevity has its place. But for me it doesn't really
matter, I only want to do God's will. And God has
allowed me to go up to the mountain top, and I have
looked over, and I have seen the Promised Land. I may
not get there with you, but I want you to know tonight,
that as a People, we shall get to the Promised Land.*

Those words were spoken by the prophet Dr. Martin
Luther King on the night before he was assassinated in
Memphis, Tennessee in the United States of America.
The Promised Land to which he was referring was a
future United States of America which would be living
the creed defined for it by those who had founded it as
a nation: 'We hold these truths to be self-evident, that
all men are created equal, that they are endowed by
their Creator with certain unalienable Rights, that
among these are Life, Liberty and the pursuit of
Happiness'. In such a Promised Land, black men and
women and other people of colour would take their
place equally alongside all others at every level of
society and in every sphere of activity.

3

The biblical history on which he was drawing was the history of the Hebrew people. They had been slaves in Egypt, living in the segregated area of Goshen, and suffering every kind of injustice at the hands of the Egyptians. There came a time when there was a man who had grown up among the privileged classes of Egypt with all the advantages of such an upbringing, but he was really of Hebrew ancestry. On a visit to the slave area he had seen an Egyptian maltreating a Hebrew and intervened to protect the victim and the Egyptian was killed. He had to flee from Egyptian reprisal and made his home among the Hebrews. But God called on him to come out of hiding and to go to the Egyptian rulers, and in the name of the Hebrew God, to demand that the Hebrews should be allowed to leave Egypt to live as a free people in a land promised to them by their God. The man's name was Moses, and he led the Hebrew people out of slavery in Egypt. The journey to the Promised Land was a long one, over many generations. But before he died, God granted him a vision of what the Promised Land was like. He was on a mountain top in the desert when God granted Moses that vision.

The Bible tells us that Moses was forty years old when he exchanged the comfortable life of an Egyptian for a life among God's people in their affliction as slaves. It also tells us that the journey to the Promised Land took forty years. But the term 'forty years' in biblical usage really means 'in the fullness of time'. In the fullness of time Moses had become a servant of God, a member of the Hebrew tribe, God's people. In the fullness of time, God's people had reached Canaan, the Promised Land.

Martin Luther King spoke his prophetic words in the year of 1968. This year, 2008, has seen Barack Obama, a black American, elected President of the United States of America, an intervening period of forty years. In the fullness of time. This is the same United States of America some of us saw on television in the early sixties. We watched as in the southern states of the USA black people lined up at the Voter Registration stations in protest against the denial to them of the right to vote. I saw clothes torn off black people by the powerful water hoses which had been turned on these peaceful demonstrators; I saw trained dogs savage people; I saw students have chairs broken on their heads and shoulders for sitting at lunch counters where service was refused. Today's USA is not yet the Promised Land of racial harmony and true brotherhood, but it is on the way, and we believe that in the fullness of time, it will become what is meant to be. But there is still a long way to go. And as with the Hebrews on their way to the Promised Land there were those who wanted to turn back, and others who lost faith in the God of Moses, so there were those who predicted that America was not ready for a black President, there will be those whose limited vision questions God's power and doubts His assurances. There but for the grace of God go we.

Today in many countries of the Commonwealth, including Barbados, Remembrance Sunday is being observed. On the second Sunday in November each year there are Church services and other observances to remember those who have died in war. The purpose is that we should not forget the cost in human lives, the waste of human potential that war demands, and to make us determined that there should be an end to war. And yet as we speak there are wars raging in Iraq, Afghanistan, the Sudan, the Congo, Sri Lanka and civil disturbances in many places all costing millions of lives. It is not surprising that some people think there is no God.

But to us, and millions of others like us assembled in

places of worship around the world today, has been given the gift of faith. Our faith tells us that whatever may be the outward signs of calamity and disintegration, there exists a God who is the union of Absolute Power and Complete Goodness, a living and loving God. We identify Him as the God, who, in the fullness of time, delivered His people from the slavery of Egypt. We identify Him as God, who, in the fullness of time sent His Son into this world gone wrong, to redeem Humankind by the sacrifice of His own life. It is this Son, known to us as Jesus the Christ, who challenges us to believe in the good purposes of God, and in Himself as the Incarnation of this God. If we accept this challenge then we must know that in the fullness of time the world will know that Christ's cry from the cross 'Tetelestai it is finished!' was a cry of victory: it is completed, victory is assured.

It is in this faith that we know that this world which is God's creation, is destined, in the fullness of time, to reflect His own loving character, that men shall study war no more; that figuratively, and perhaps literally, the lion will lie down with the lamb, and they shall neither hurt nor destroy for the earth will be filled with the glory of God, as the waters cover the sea.

You and I may not live to enter that Promised Land. But that we have lived to see the election of a black president of the most powerful nation on earth means that God has allowed us all, black and white, men and women, young and old, rich and poor, gay and straight, Jew and Gentile, native and immigrant, Muslim, Hindu, Buddhist and people of every creed, if not to go up to the mountain top then at least to stand on the tip-toe of faith and look over the fence of scepticism and cynicism, to catch glimpses of the Promised Land, which only awaits the fullness of time. This is the faith of the Church. This is our faith.

2
Life Experience With Britain

Talk given at the George Padmore Institute, London, UK
chaired by John La Rose, 19 April 1999

Mr Chairman, Ladies and Gentlemen, I am highly
appreciative of the honour accorded me by the
invitation to give this talk and this is no mere pleasantry
on my part, because I know that the discriminating
perceptiveness of John La Rose and Sarah White has
not diminished one jot over their long years of active,
steadfast commitment to social justice and universal
human rights. So to be asked by them and their
colleagues in the George Padmore Institute to share
my thoughts in a forum of this kind is no mean
accolade. I thank them and apologise in advance if my
contribution falls short of expectations. I also take this
opportunity to salute them for their contribution to a
better world for all us, a contribution which will be
valued long after we have all passed on. Mr Chairman,
I have been asked in this talk to cover a) my origins in
Barbados, b) my social experience as a progressive in
British society and c) my experience in the Church of
England, on being exalted to becoming its first black
bishop. It is perhaps a more self-centred assignment
than would be my preference, but I will do my best.

In 1951, parliamentary elections to the twenty-four
seat House of Assembly in Barbados with its twelve
double-member constituencies, were held on adult
suffrage basis, that is everyone aged twenty-one and
over being able to vote, for the first time. My father,
Wilfred Coward, a small businessman managing his
own Boston Bus Company and sitting as a vestryman,
which was equivalent of a borough councillor, in St

John La Rose in the George Padmore Institute Photo Armet Francis

Joseph, was persuaded to stand as a candidate for the Planters and Merchants Party – then known as the Electors' Association – against the two sitting members from the Barbados Labour Party, Mr Grantley Adams, who was in fact the leader of the party, and Mr Lloyd Smith, a local shopkeeper. I was only a fifteen year-old schoolboy at Combermere School at the time but I became very interested and each night I was out at the various public meetings. One night after my father had made his speech and left the lorry platform to mingle with the crowd, I persuaded the chairman to let me say a few words. It went down so well that I became a regular speaker, usually just before my father came on. To be honest, ours was not a popular cause – my father was soundly defeated – but I can still recall that at the final meeting there was an enormous crowd, mostly hostile, when I went to the microphone. The growling crowd stilled when I announced, 'Let me compare for you, my father and Mr Grantley Adams.' I went on, 'For east is east and west is west, and ne'er the twain shall meet; 'til earth and sky stand presently at God's good judgement sat but there is neither east nor west, border nor breed nor birth, when two strong men stand face to face, though they came from the ends of the earth.' At the words, 'when two strong men' there was such a deafening roar that I had to pause and repeat it because I would have been lynched if I had have said anything against Adams. I can tell you that.

As I said, we were soundly beaten. Adams and Smith were returned, the Labour Party formed the government with a sound majority, the cobbled-together Electors' Association fell apart, later re-emerging as the Progressive Conservatives. I remember some chap seeing a man walk up and down Broad Street and he said, 'Well he must be a Progressive Conservative. He doesn't know if he's walking forwards or backwards.' Having become seriously interested in politics though, my father joined the Labour Party and at subsequent elections we both spoke in support of various Labour candidates. Ten years after those momentous 1951 elections, my father was elected to sit alongside Mr Smith. Mr Adams had gone off to become the first and only Prime Minister of the ill-fated West Indies Federation. There is an amusing footnote to all this. In 1966 here in London, one of Mr Smith's six daughters – Ina – and I were married. So our five children have the unique distinction of being the only people to have had two grandfathers representing the same constituency at the same time.

You will understand that, having caught the eye of Sir Grantley Adams, I was set fair for a political career, and indeed I had decided that I would be a journalist and politician. Meanwhile, like many other people I was regular in church on Sundays, I read the Bible and said my prayers just like most people. While I was growing up, the local parish priest, the Reverend J. T. Adams-Cooper was a Glaswegian Scot, and as far as I know only one woman in the entire parish – the verger – understood anything he said! He retired and was succeeded by a young priest from St Vincent who took an interest in the young people and drew me more into the life of the church. So I found myself helping with the Sunday School, running the Church Lads' Brigade, being drill instructor to the Church Girls' Brigade and the darling of the elderly matrons to whom I sometimes gave a lift to and from church.

Woody Allen, the film maker and comedian, has said, 'If you really want to make God laugh, try planning your own life.' Well, I came to realise, with complete conviction, that God was calling me to be a priest. Since I definitely did not want to be a priest – the life did not appeal to me – and since I already knew what I wanted to do with my life, I convinced myself that I could not rise to the high standards which God would rightly expect of a priest and it was better to be a good layman than a bad priest, so I redoubled all my church work and I shared my thoughts with no one. Then, on 7 July 1957, the Bishop, whose name was Gay Lisle Griffith Mandeville so he rejoiced in the title Gay Barbados, came for confirmation to our church of St Anne, and in the course of his remarks about God's call and our response, quoting an older priest he said, 'If God calls on you to jump through a brick wall, it is your duty to jump. It is God's business to see you through.' After that I had to have the matter resolved. So I was then seen by the bishop, archdeacon, dean, the principal of Codrington College and the headmaster of Harrison College, often, frankly, in a rather questioning and rebellious frame of mind, but the result was that I embarked on a five-year training for the priesthood at Codrington College.

Now we do not have time for a proper description of my time at Codrington College. But I can say that I fell in love with the person of Jesus Christ and knew then that my overriding purpose in life, so far as was humanly possible, was to be faithful to what I came to know of Him. There was no need to grasp at anything – riches, success, acclaim, not even the priesthood itself. Whatever brick walls there were, provided He said jump, I knew what was expected of me. Now I am no Billy Graham, and even if I were, this is not a revivalist meeting, but it still remains true that, in spite of the many charlatans who see Christianity as a safe and easy way to make a quick buck, or of wielding power over gullible and vulnerable people, the call to love as Jesus loves, embracing as it does a recognition of yourself as someone of infinite worth, and yet no more so and no less so than other people for whom Christ was prepared to give His life, that is the true liberation.

I was still a student at Codrington College along with others from Anguilla, St Kitts, Nevis, Saba, how many of you know there's a West Indian island called Saba? Antigua, St Vincent, Grenada, Trinidad, Guyana, Tobago, Bermuda, the Bahamas, the UK and Barbados when the West Indies Federation broke up. I remember it well because, contrary to the rules of the College, we used to assemble in the darkness during the night to listen to test match cricket from Australia, and on the first occasion when the West Indies won, a Trinidadian – who incidentally is now a vicar in Wembley – mounted a small West Indian flag on a broomstick and we marched around in a circle singing, 'West Indian boys are marching.' I then sat down and wrote a National

Anthem for the West Indies and some years later it was sent back to me with a sad little note saying, that with the break up of the Federation, there was now no requirement for an anthem.

Because I was paying my own fees at Codrington College, or to be more accurate, my father was paying them, I was not under obligation to any diocese, and in 1959 came the news of the disturbances in Notting Hill and the death of Kelso Cochrane, murdered by teddy boys. Now, one feature of the ministry of Jesus that appealed strongly to me was that, although he spoke straight from the shoulder, as it were, to rich and poor alike, His message was that they belonged together. I was brought up in Barbados with a very idealised image of Britain – not unlike John Major's old ladies cycling to Holy Communion, village green cricket with polite applause and murmurs of 'Good shot, old boy', a bastion of fair play and British pride, where 'of all the world's great heroes there's none that can compare, with a tow-row-row-row-row row of the British grenadier'. Indeed I was interested to read in the *Guardian* six days ago, an interview with Trevor Hicks who lost two daughters in the Hillsborough Football Stadium disaster ten years ago. He said and I quote, 'Where I came from, it was hard work and play it straight and you'll get on eventually. Britain was the fairest country in the world; there was room for everyone to have their say and what you read in the papers was dead right.' That was also the view that, I, living in Barbados, had of Britain. Hicks went on to say, 'What a load of bollocks!'

So, when we heard that the cause of the trouble was the failure of West Indians now living in Britain to respect the rights of English people to sleep at night when the West Indians preferred to have noisy parties, and their refusal to queue for buses and so on, I felt ashamed that our people who had gone to England were letting the side down. So I volunteered to go to England after ordination for a period of four years to show the West Indians a better way, before returning to Barbados. I saw this as something of a sacrifice because, although the Government (by now E.W. Barrow's Democratic Labour Party) had intimated that the Church would be disestablished, the clergy in Barbados still enjoyed all the privileges of service in a church in which government paid for everything – from clergy stipends to communion wafers – and there were still such things as long-leave passages every four years. So the Mirfield Fathers – that's the Community of Resurrection, who staffed Codrington College at the time – gave me their blessing and made arrangements for me to serve my title with one of their former students, Roderick Gibbs, who was then a Vicar of St Stephen's, Shepherd's Bush. So on 19th July 1962 I embarked on the *Golfito*, arrived at Avonmouth on 6th August and Paddington Station on 7th August.

Some of you will remember, even more clearly than I do, the London of those days. Many features which are commonplace today – underpasses and elevated motorways, central heating, modern office blocks, grime-free houses and so on had not yet arrived. Living conditions for most black people – mainly West Indians and Africans with some Asians – meant one room which had to be bedroom, living room, dressing room everything for both parents and children, sharing a cooker on the dark landing with a number of other families similarly ill-housed. Often the heating was provided by a paraffin heater which meant that one's clothes smelt always of paraffin. My first experience of an English winter was that of 1962 with the last great London smog, when for a whole week you could not see for more than a yard or two around you. I used to go visiting with another curate who was a bit of a wag and he would say, 'Look, can you keep smiling so I can see where you are.'

The English people with whom I had to do were magnificent, and they could not have been kinder. I lived with the vicar, his wife Joan and three little daughters, Monica, Paula and Lucy, in the rambling Victorian vicarage, very much as one of the family. I know this sounds like a cliché, but you really must trust my honesty when I tell you that this was really so and that I will never be able to repay them. There were other members of the church also, mostly solid working class people. There was, for example, the factory manager Bert James, with his motorcycle and sidecar. With me on the pillion and, believe it or not, his wife and three small children in the sidecar. We would travel to places like Windsor Great Park, Frensham Ponds, Guildford Cathedral, Coventry, Stratford-upon-Avon and so on. Then there was the elderly, retired spinster, Mabel Voller, who had been in domestic service all her life and who took me under her wing. When I married she took my wife also, and when the children came along, one, two, three, four, she took them as well. She was a wonderful person, fiercely loyal to royalty and the Conservative Party. 'Go home Dick Feather!' she would hiss at the trade union leader, Vic Feather, whenever he appeared on television. She would compare white babies unfavourably with our own and then say with a wry smile, 'Makes me feel like a traitor to me own kind.' Even before I arrived, black people had been made to feel welcome in that particular church. I'll tell you a story about Mabel Voller. One day I was in a bookshop, church bookshop in Oxford Street and saw a book *Little Black Sambo* and I got so embarrassed and asked, 'Are you still selling these books?' I bought it to take home and to write to protest about it. I took it home and put it down and one day came back to find Mabel reading it to our little daughter who was enjoying it enormously!

But for most black people church-going was a luxury. Shift work and having to share essential domestic facilities with so many others meant that they were not really in control of their lives. In addition many of those arriving in the 1950s or earlier had had very bad experiences of rejection when they turned up at church, only to find people draw away from them as though they were contagious. So they had resorted to reading their bibles at home, eventually joining others to pray together. Many black churches began in this way. I became increasingly dissatisfied with a ministry to people's spiritual needs which seemed to ignore their obvious physical needs, and I raised this with the vicar. He sympathised with my anxieties but thought that I should first have a proper grounding in the bread-and-butter aspects of parish ministry, supporting people in funerals, weddings, baptisms and illness, before tackling social and political action. The bishop agreed with him so I continued my ministry, still intending to return to the Caribbean at the end of my four years.

It was not easy to buckle down to this discipline. Harold Macmillan's Conservative government was on its last legs, and eventually an election was called in 1964 and Labour under Harold Wilson won a tiny, single-figure majority. But it was a turning-point election. One of the Labour Party's most senior and respected figures who was destined to be the Foreign Secretary, Patrick Gordon-Walker, was ousted from the safe Labour seat of Smethwick by an otherwise unknown teacher named Peter Griffiths, whose campaign featured such slogans as, 'If you want a Nigger for a neighbour, vote Labour'. The Labour government took fright. Too many of their politicians had waited long for their turn in government and were not prepared to miss out over this issue. There was no difference between them, Left or Right, you have only to hear tapes or read transcripts of their answers on phone-ins to spot their unease. Since everyone knew that with such a slender majority a second election was likely, there developed an auction between the two major parties, each striving to show that they would be as tough on 'immigration', which was really a code word for the presence of black people, as the other.

It so happened that the defeated Conservative candidate in my constituency of North Hammersmith was a man called Tom Stacey, who was a journalist and wrote for the *Sunday Times*. He wrote a piece entitled, 'The Ghettoes of England'. I still have it, and in it, by the clever use of words, he purported to show that the prejudices against black people actually had a factual basis. For example, he wrote that he could always tell an immigrant street such as Coningham Road, which happened to be in my parish. He said that the houses would be dilapidated, the front area would be strewn with debris, the windows would be broken and so on. What he did not say was that Coningham Road, with Stowe Road and Cathnor Road on either side, were all of a piece, but that Coningham Road was the only one with black people. He also said that knocking on the doors throughout the day, he found more black men disproportionately home on the dole than white. I knew that often I paid baptism visits and had to speak to the wife while the husband was a bundle under the blankets because he was working nights, and so on and so on. I wrote to the *Sunday Times* complaining and trying to correct the misleading statements. They preferred to publish two short letters, one agreeing with Stacey and the other disagreeing. But I noted that the one in agreement they had chosen was from Barons Court not far away, while the one disagreeing was from someone living in Malta. Quite fair, you see!

Labour did win the second election with a proper working majority and I wrote to and got an appointment with Maurice Foley, the Minister in the Home Office responsible for immigration and race relations. His view was that no special action was needed, because, as people saw how good black people were at their jobs, they would be educated into tolerance. So a black doctor had only to be a good doctor, a black priest a good priest and so on. I was not convinced. The only entry in the telephone directory with race relations in the title was the Institute of Race Relations at 36 Jermyn Street near Piccadilly. So I went to see its director, Philip Mason. Alas, he explained, it was not that kind of project. This was an academic institute concerned with research and study rather than action. What I had in mind at this time was the establishment of a kind of Toynbee Hall in Shepherd's Bush. There was on the Uxbridge Road going towards Acton an army building which had been empty and unused for years, which I thought would be ideal. Youngsters who had no space at home to do homework properly could come there for that as well as recreation and vocational activities. It contained living quarters so university students could come to help the youngsters in the neighbourhood. I wrote to various politicians who had liberal reputations but none could help. One answered asking how did I know this was what black people wanted. This was Jo Grimond who was a great liberal. I did manage to see an official in the Ministry of Defence. He explained that there were plans to rebuild the Duke of York's headquarters in Chelsea and this building may be needed during that time. Years later the headquarters were indeed rebuilt but the Shepherd's Bush building was never used and remained unoccupied.

When in 1964 the Wilson government tried to appease the racists by imposing an arbitrary limit on the number of immigrants per year to be allowed in to take up jobs, and claimed to be doing it in the best interest of race relations, it also set up the National Committee for Commonwealth Immigrants (NCCI), to create a network of local Community Relations Councils. These councils could only be set up with the support of the local authority, who had to provide half of the officer's £1500-a-year salary if the local Community Relations Council was to be recognised by the NCCI. For the most part those borough councils which did respond ensured that the price of their co-operation was control by them. Nonetheless this was the only thing on offer, so I became chairman of the Hammersmith Council for Community Relations. Kensington and Chelsea Borough Council refused to have such a council, so a few of us set up a voluntary group and appointed James Cummings as its first full-time officer. These councils were not an overnight success. Local authority support was grudging. The lone officer, usually called the liaison officer, was often inadequately supported and spent most of his time explaining to needy immigrants why he could not meet their expectations. However, we limped on.

Meanwhile in the wider world the race issue was unfolding. The apartheid regime in South Africa was becoming even more brutal, having jailed Nelson Mandela and his colleagues. Rhodesia was moving in the same direction. Black Power was emerging in the USA and the Kenyan government had put its Asian residents on notice to choose between British citizenship and Kenyan citizenship. White racists abroad and in Britain were receiving influential support and the Wilson government was running with the hares and hunting with the hounds. Multi-ethnic groups campaigning for a genuine multi-ethnic society and strong legislation against racist practices and discrimination were definitely not the flavour of the month.

For some of us matters came to a head when the Asians were expelled from Kenya and the government rushed through overnight legislation to deprive them of British citizenship and the right to enter Britain. By remarkable coincidence at the very same time the Russian troops were massing to break up the movement in Czechoslovakia and the British Consul there was open around the clock to process as many Czechs who wanted to escape and come to Britain as possible, the British Consul in Nairobi was open for one hour only for passports for those few who could get passports in that hour, while the legislation was going through to deprive them of the right to come here. That was all in the same twenty-four hours.

Anyway, this exposed the NCCI to be the government's fig leaf that it was, since it had not been consulted and its advice ignored. I contacted two chairmen of neighbouring Community Relations Councils who, like me, happened to be black, and we called a Sunday afternoon meeting in our church hall in Shepherd's Bush of as many councils as we could contact. The idea was for these councils to stay together but independent of the government-control led and discredited NCCI, and so form the nucleus of a civil rights movement. The NCCI got hold of the plan and called a meeting two days before, paying the train fares and hotel accommodation of representatives to attend the meeting, which was a major consideration for those coming from the North and Midlands and we didn't have money to do the same. They solicited their support and sent them back home disinclined to have anything to do with our insurrection.

However, that did not deter us and later, when the government was debating the replacing of the NCCI by a Community Relations Commission, which was eventually headed by Frank Cousins, we submitted what came to be known as 'The Wood Proposals', in which we called for a Committee for Racial Equality. In those days the idea of equality was un-thought of. You couldn't mention it in decent company. You could have integration, yes, or harmony or community relations, but the idea of equality, that wasn't on at all. Anyway we called for a Committee for Racial Equality with membership at least in part directly elected from immigrant organisations and, what is more located, not in the Home Office with its concerns for immigration, prisons and Police, public disorder and so on, but in either the Department of Local Government or the Department of Education and Science. Needless to say the Home Secretary, James Callaghan, and his minister, David Ennals, ignored these proposals. Powellism was now flexing its muscles and appeasement was the order of the day.

On the church front there were a number of individual Christians who stood by their fellow black Christians. But, in spite of tireless work from people like Rev'd John Downing, Rev'd Lewis Donnelly, Rev'd Alex Kirby, Rev'd David Haslam, Canon John Collins, Bishop Trevor Huddleston, Douglas Tilby, a Quaker, and Michael and Ann Dummett, the Church as a whole had no appetite for public opposition to the Government and the rising tide of racism. Certainly I can remember church meetings at which people took exception to my call to condemn Powell and some even walked out. It became clear to me that, although there was a place for friendship meetings and tea parties for black and white people to learn more about one another, effective pushing for justice and equality would have to come from us, the black people, ourselves.

So I made a point of attending the monthly meeting at the West Indian Students Centre in Earls Court of the West Indian Standing Conference. The chairman at the time was Neville Maxwell, and its secretary Jeff Crawford. Neville Maxwell was a law lecturer with an extremely fine brain, he was a former Barbados scholar, a man of vision with that rare gift, the common touch. He was a true leader who made allowances for the limitations of those he was trying to lead, and it is not necessarily disparaging to say that those limitations were severe. I remember John here had a regular spot where he gave an erudite round-up of political activity in the Caribbean, but truth to tell the meetings were usually a talk-shop of empty rhetoric where nothing happened and nothing was expected to happen. I remember one person, who shall be nameless, seriously proposing a resolution calling on the Soviet Union to come to the aid of black people in Britain. When I proposed that individual membership should be drastically reduced in order to encourage people to build up affiliated organisations and work through them, and that the monthly meeting should be hosted by member organisations in turn, with the members of that organisation having the right to form a 'public gallery', it was turned down.

That is not to say that West Indian Standing Conference achieved nothing. Joe Hunte's little pamphlet, 'Nigger-hunting in London', drew public attention to police harassment and mistreatment of black people and the campaign to force London Transport to appoint black bus inspectors was successful. Jeff Crawford was an effective secretary and credit for much of what was achieved must go to him. I must say I was very disappointed that in all the great hoo haa about the *Windrush*, the programmes on television and so on, very little mention, in fact no mention was made of Jeff Crawford, and he played a crucial part in those days. I still have a 1968 *Guardian* photograph of him and me picketing London Transport's offices with placards demanding an end to their discrimination. I also remember, because it's written deep in my mind, on that day when we were going to picket those offices at St James, in fact I had been ill in bed with a heavy cold. It was in March, I think, and the weather was quite bad and I got out of bed and was muffled up with lots of scarves and coats and so on. Standing up there with this placard and all the time feeling extremely angry that if I were to get my death of cold, what would I have died for, to have a man made, of all things, a bus inspector?

But self-help had to be bottom-up rather than top-down. So in 1967, after a series of meetings in our home, twelve of us from Barbados, Grenada, Jamaica and Guyana founded the Shepherd's Bush Social and Welfare Association and set about building up a membership. The Reverend John Asbridge, who had succeeded Roderick Gibbs as vicar of St Stephen with St Thomas, was sympathetic and helpful and supported us in obtaining St Thomas Hall, Thornfield Road, for our activities. We were able to get a supplementary school going, and employed one of our own members, Clinton Sealy, to run the school as well as to accompany parents when they had occasion to visit schools in connection with their children's education and welfare. We went on to found the Shepherd's Bush Credit Union and, despite the hostility of one resident in particular who took us to court, claiming a noise nuisance, the Association is still going and there is a full-time day nursery on the premises.

The Reverend John Asbridge persuaded me to join the local Rotary Club and together we challenged them, as persons whose businesses flourished in Shepherd's Bush because of the presence of black people, to show practical concern for their customers. So began the Shepherd's Bush Housing Association with a committee made up of the vicar, church wardens and me, and a number of people we had recruited, with my wife doing the secretarial work on the church's typewriter and Gestetner copier, all unpaid of course, supported by the local Rotary Club. I remember helping to lay the lino – no carpet in those days – when we secured our first house and moved in a Jamaican family as our first tenants. Since then the Association has gone on to own just under 3,000 properties and to house thousands of families. I was much moved when a few years ago they asked me to return to Shepherd's Bush to open Wilfred Wood Court. In self-help housing I joined Pansy Jeffreys and others to found the Berbice Co-operative Housing Association, and Lee Samuel and others to found Carib Housing Association, which has so far provided four sheltered housing schemes for elderly Caribbean people, where every resident has a fully self-contained flat with bedroom, sitting-room, kitchen, toilet and bath and so on and yet has access to communal facilities whenever they wish to use them. One of them is here in North London and is called Clive Lloyd House.

It was around this time that the bishop decided that the experience I had acquired would be more beneficial to the Church in this country than in the Caribbean and created a post for me equivalent to that of a vicar. I became bishop's officer in Race Relations which gave me the freedom to concentrate on those issues which I thought were important for the Church's contribution to a genuine multi-ethnic, multi-cultural society in this country. The rough deal which black people were receiving at the hands of the Police and the courts was presented sharply to me in two incidents at that time.

One Sunday afternoon a Grenadian member of our congregation came to ask me to come with him to get his uncle out of Shepherd's Bush police station. His uncle's story was that the night before in a crowded pub he was trying to get the bartender to change a ten pound note for him. A man who was nearer the bar passed the money to the barman, but instead of passing the change back to the West Indian, put it in his pocket and started to make his way out. The West Indian grabbed him and asked for the police to be called. The police arrived and promptly arrested the West Indian, took him off to the station and charged him with being drunk and disorderly. After retrieving him from the cells that Sunday afternoon I phoned a solicitor who was unable to appear in court next day, but advised him to ask for an adjournment of two weeks and to apply for legal aid after pleading not guilty. As Monday, the next day, was my day off, I was able to accompany him to the West London Magistrates Court. I don't know if you've ever been in a Magistrates Court on a Monday morning but there is a kind of conveyor belt of persons pleading guilty to being drunk and disorderly. A chap comes up, 'John Jones you are charged with being drunk and disorderly. Do you plead guilty or not guilty?' 'Guilty Sir.' 'Ten pounds.' This goes on all the time. Then in comes my man. 'You're charged with being drunk and disorderly. Do you plead guilty or not guilty?' He said, 'Not guilty.' The magistrate (almost annoyed) 'Not guilty?' The clerk says, 'He's asked for legal aid.' 'Legal aid for an offence where the fine is only about ten pounds? No, no. not granted.' 'He's asked for an adjournment of two weeks.' 'Why do you want an adjournment of two weeks?' 'My solicitor ...'. 'You've got a solicitor?' 'Yes, Sir.' 'What's his name?' My man says the name. 'Yes he is a solicitor. Alright, one week. If he were interested he would be here. One week.' I was sitting watching and as it turned out in the end he was acquitted on a technicality, because it was clear that he had been arrested in the pub whereas the charge had been drunk and disorderly in the street.

Soon after that I was called by another West Indian parishioner to Hammersmith police station on a Friday evening to retrieve a young man who had been at my home only the previous Sunday. This was a guy that I knew quite well because I had baptised his baby not very long before and he had had to go home to Grenada because his mother had died. While he was there the priest who was taking the funeral had asked him to remember him to me when he came back. He was writing a thank you letter to the priest and realised that he hadn't done that and left off writing the letter and came around just to do that. So that was a Sunday. On the Friday evening his cousin came to ask if I would get him out of the police cells and I was surprised because he was not that type of person. This is what had happened. He was a motor mechanic and he owned a Morris Minor and he had seen outside a house in Ravensbourne Road a similar car which had been involved in an accident and was obviously a write-off. So he'd made enquiries and discovered it was owned by the people outside whose house it was standing, and arranged to buy the engine from them. This evening after work he had gone to them, told them he was going to work on the car and started work on the car. He was hammering the grille away when he felt someone grab him by the collar, jerk him upright and this young man saying, 'You black bastards can't keep your hands off other people's property. I am arresting you for stealing parts from this car.' So the chap who had done this was about his size and the West Indian chap started to really lay into him. Then a uniformed policeman saw this and came running and said, 'You can't treat a police officer like that!' He explained to this policeman in uniform what had happened and he said, 'Well, we'll see if he's telling the truth.' Took him, rang the door bell and the woman said, 'What are you doing to this young man? I gave him permission to take the engine.' 'Oh,' said the first policeman, 'In that case I charge you with using an offensive weapon,' which was the hammer that he had been using to hammer the grille with.

So once more I contacted the solicitor. At the trial the Police offered no evidence and the case was dismissed. The magistrate was quite annoyed actually. I was highly indignant at what the young man and his family had been made to go through and the expense, and I wanted to sue the Police for damages. But the solicitor explained that once we started bringing actions against the Police, acquittals would be that much harder to obtain so it was better to let the matter drop.

So I was glad, realising all this, to accept an invitation to address four meetings of police personnel, around 200 at a time, on their dealings with the immigrant community. The hostile reaction which greeted the five mild suggestions with which I concluded my talk is instructive. I still have, I meant to bring it actually, a tape of that talk. I gave it on four occasions. For example, the five suggestions I made. I suggested there should be black policemen and the answer was, 'Why should we lower our standards?' I suggested that as professionals they should make it their business to know something of the culture and background of the people they were policing and they said, 'We are not social workers.' I suggested that they should first warn the immigrant when he is seen to be breaking the law as he might not know he is breaking the law and they said, 'We are here to enforce the law.' I suggested to them that the men and women who are on the beat now should be relaying their experiences to their superior officers, in order to educate those for whom immigrants were not a feature of the population when they were on the beat and they said, 'That's not our business.' I suggested that it was misplaced loyalty to support colleagues who mistreat black people. It was very interesting those talks.

I remember they would get quite steamed up actually, the police, about this and I remember one policeman saying, because we had questions and answers afterwards, 'I think the trouble is that you black people don't have a sense of humour.' So I said to him, 'How many black friends do you have whose houses you go to?' He said, 'None.' 'Black people coming to your house?' 'No, no, no.' I said, ' Now you just heard me speak for about forty minutes. Would you say I haven't got a sense of humour?' He said, 'Yeah, but you're different.' Another time a policeman said, he was absolutely livid with anger, he said, 'You tell me, why is it that when you arrest a black man and take him to court, he always pleads not guilty?' I said, 'It may be because he isn't guilty.' I mean, even the other policemen found that funny. They laughed.

I was also glad to work with the late Brother Herman Edwards in his efforts to help young people who had fallen foul of the Police and as a result had become alienated from parents who, with attitudes brought from the Caribbean, assumed that the youngsters must have done something to bring it upon themselves. So we founded Harambee and Herman now lives on in the lives of the many young people he rescued from a life of crime and helped to make good.

All this showed me how crucial to a future harmonious multi-ethnic society would be the proper functioning of the Police and the justice system, so I was pleased to be appointed a Justice of the Peace. I have no doubt at all that my presence on the Magistrate's Bench made a difference in a number of individual cases and to the enlightenment of fellow magistrates in matters relating to black people. Incidentally, it's the only occasion I've been called, 'Your Majesty' and that was, we had this case which came up, a West Indian, a Jamaican chap had an old car and he had bought another car. The first car he had was no good, he'd bought another one and he had transferred the disc from the old car to the new one which isn't legal really, shouldn't do it and a policewoman who had gone down the street looking at the various discs had decided to charge him. He saw her and explained to her what he'd done but she was determined to do him and he was charged. He came to court and explained that he'd been living in this country almost thirty years, he had never been in trouble with the Police and he had no intention of cheating and so on. It seemed obvious to me that what he was really concerned about was the loss of his good name, that he'd got himself in trouble and so on. So when we retired I explained all this to the other magistrate and we decided that he would be given an absolute discharge. Because the offence was actually committed he couldn't deny it. He had actually done that but this was a device where, as it were, no guilt is attached, you see, to be given an absolute discharge. So when we came out I explained this to him that there would be no stain on his character, he would not have to pay anything, there'd be no offence registered or anything. He was so delighted he backed out of the court, bowing and saying, 'Thank you, Your Majesty, thank you, Your Majesty, thank you, Your Majesty.'

This in turn led to my appointment to the Royal Commission on Criminal Procedure, which was set up in 1978 in the wake of the Confait case by the Callaghan government, and which reported three years later to the Thatcher government. The Commission recommended the setting up of the Crown Prosecution Service to replace the system where Police were both investigators and prosecutors, and also recommended certain criteria that had to be met if an arrest was to be made. Now my membership of that Commission provided me with a number of interesting experiences. For example, I remember a Ditchley Park Conference in 1978 attended by more than thirty police chief constables and some American law enforcement officers including a deputy director of the FBI. This was in 1978 and the theme of the conference was 'Policing in the 1990s'. The FBI's representative confessed that in the USA they had learned their lessons too late so far as the inner cities were concerned. What people in the inner city wanted were reliable and trustworthy Police who could be counted on to do their job professionally. To do them credit, the majority of chief constables favoured this approach, so they paid little attention to the lone voice who argued that it was the Northern Ireland experience that had provided the pattern for future policing in Britain's inner cities. However, with the change of government came the time for a successor to Sir David McNee, Metropolitan Police Commissioner and it was this man, Sir Kenneth Newman, who was appointed. The rest is history.

By and large the baleful influence of Enoch Powell made sure that the highest aspiration of officialdom was racial quiet rather than racial justice and, needless to say, it was the victims who paid the price for this quiet. The race relations debate was really between two groups of people, the Powellites and the liberals, with no real attention paid to the wishes or opinions of the black community. It did not help that self-appointed, so-called Black Power activists went around disrupting meetings of any black groups of whom they disapproved. One legacy of such madness is a generation of black people who have fallen victims to the individualistic self-interest quest for personal fame, wealth and power characteristic of the Thatcher era. In spite of this, I do not believe that all is lost.

Now let me share with you two personal incidents that have been quite influential on my own thinking. Some of you may remember the 1963 all-conquering West Indies cricket team which toured England led by Frank Worrell. It was a team that would have beaten any other team in the world. It had the two fastest bowlers of the time, Wes Hall and Charlie Griffiths; the best off-spinner of the time, Lance Gibbs; the most brilliant batsman, Rohan Kanhai; and above all, a unique, one-off cricketer who could bowl both fast-medium and swing and left-arm spin at test-match level and who held the record for the world's highest individual test score, Garfield Sobers. That team would have beaten anybody. I happened to be visiting our scouts in camp at a time when this team had beaten England yet again, and was engaging in banter about this with the scout master when I heard one of the scouts, who I knew to be keen and knowledgeable about cricket, turn aside and mutter, 'England beaten by a bunch of niggers!' Now if you come from Barbados you know that cricket is a religion. So it registered with me then that for some people it does not matter how much of a genius a black person may be, no matter how many inventions, doctorates, Nobel prizes, heroic feats and so on may be attributed to him, for such people he is first and foremost a nigger. Now, such people may never be in a majority but however much we regret that they do exist, they do, and it is really silly and even dangerous to pretend that they do not.

The second incident occurred in 1967 after I had made a broadcast on the BBC. Some weeks later there was a knock on our door in Bloemfontein Avenue, Shepherd's Bush and I found a young man and a very old man, both black, standing there. The old man was completely blind but he had heard me on the radio and made his way all the way from Cardiff to my home. He had been a follower of Marcus Garvey in his youth and he held me in a tight and emotional embrace. 'There used to be thousands of black people in this country,' he said in a voice trembling with emotion, 'Where are they now? Don't let it happen again. Don't let it happen again.' It is my view that ethnic identification in this country will follow the pattern which can be recognised in the United States of America. First there are the genuine immigrants, people who arrive in the country with their own cultural values and practices. Children born to them in the new country are apt to want more than anything else to be just like their peers, that is, to be normal. They tend to be half-ashamed of their parents' way of speaking, and sometimes dressing or dietary preferences. It seems backward to them. They rarely invite their friends to their homes, much preferring to visit them in theirs. However, it is the second and subsequent generations who are keenly interested in their grandparents and are most proud of their roots and the other identity they have in addition to that which comes with their place of birth. It is said that many almost fanatic 'Irish-Americans' have never set foot in Ireland nor are likely to.

So it seems to me important that black and 'double-ethnic' children – incidentally, that's the term that I'm trying to get into common use. Double-ethnic is much better than half-caste or mixed-race. You see, double-ethnic is positive. It means that you have two of what most people only have one of, you see and, what is more, you are equally proud of both. So do please use that term, double-ethnic.

Member of the audience: I have three.

Wilfred Wood: Or four or five. As I said it seems to me important that black and double-ethnic children of the future must have available to them documentary and other evidence, to show that their grandparents were not all passive receivers of scraps thrown to us, but were proud and resilient people, who, in the face of great difficulties and adversity, made possible the space in which they are now able to spread their wings. For example, whatever good may result from the Stephen Lawrence murder inquiry and whatever credit must go to the Home Secretary, Jack Straw, and Sir William MacPherson for recognising institutional racism, there have been other pointless racist murders of young black men in this country. The decisive factor in this case is the refusal of two immigrant parents, Doreen and Neville Lawrence, to accept the powerlessness which an indifferent society has decreed for them. This nation owes them a great debt.

And now you'll be pleased to hear, I'm on to the third bit. Now to my experience in the Church of England on being exalted to becoming its 'first black bishop'. This is the title given to me, by the way, I didn't choose it. You have been so indulgent an audience that it seems almost criminal to make this demand upon you, so I will be brief in this third section of my assignment. When on the 8th March 1985 I opened a letter from the Bishop of Southwark, Ronnie Bowlby, to read his invitation to become Bishop of Croydon, I handed the letter to my wife and said, 'Well, if this is the latest brick wall, here goes.' You see, ever since I had been Archdeacon of Southwark in 1982 there had been speculation that I would go on to be a bishop, since I was 46 years old then. But it was assumed that this would be somewhere with a substantial black population, and this was hardly true of Croydon. So this was a surprise for everyone, including myself.

Another reason for surprise was that I could hardly be described as a 'safe pair of hands' or an 'establishment man'. Indeed, a parishioner of mine in Catford, where I was vicar, was once attending a conference and mentioned me as the vicar of her parish. 'Wilfred Wood,' said this priest to her, 'I have heard that name. Isn't he someone with a bee in his bonnet about black people?' My parishioner replied, 'You may well have done so because there aren't that many black vicars around.' 'What?' exclaimed the priest, 'You mean he is actually black?' Another friend of mine, when he heard this story, shook his head in mock solemnity and said, 'The lengths some people will go to!' I had taken over the chairmanship of the Institute of Race Relations when its academics, politicians, bankers and industrialists had been ousted from its council and replaced with black people and activists. I had loudly and publicly opposed various racist policies and legislation, gone on various demonstrations against Ian Smith's UDI in Rhodesia and British action in Anguilla, for example, walked from New Cross to Hyde Park in the Black People's Day of Action following the New Cross fire and so on. Above all I had chaired the World Council of Churches' Programme to Combat Racism when we made grants to the liberation movements in Azania, that is South Africa, and Zimbabwe, Rhodesia as it was, to support their humanitarian work even though they were engaged in liberation wars, and when the Church of England did not lack supporters of white rule in South Africa and Rhodesia in its Assembly, that is General Synod and elsewhere. So I was hardly ideal material really for a token appointment.

But it was not a token appointment. Ronnie Bowlby is a christian firmly committed to equality and justice and made a point of informing me that he had made a list of the qualities sought in the new Bishop by those he had consulted. He could honestly say, having observed me at work as Archdeacon of Southwark, that I met them better than anyone else he knew. It was important that I should know this for myself, he said, whatever else may be read into the appointment. It made me recall being told by a parishioner that there had been some agitation at the time that it was announced that I was to be the new vicar of St Laurence, Catford. She had said to the agitators, 'Look, we've got everything we asked for. We just forgot to say that he shouldn't be black!'

You may remember my saying that my first winter in this country was the 1962 winter, which was extremely cold with the last great London smog. I enjoyed it, simply because having come expecting to be cold and miserable, it didn't much matter how cold and miserable. Well, it is in the same way that one approaches appointments of this kind. In the same way it must be recognised that there are certain inescapable conditions peculiar to all black people in leadership roles in British institutions today. I'll repeat that. There are certain conditions which are peculiar to all black people who are higher, who are at the top of leading British institutions today.

It is rather like being an undersized boy in a school playground. A physically well-built boy may be the greatest coward on earth but is never challenged to a fight, whereas every playground bully fancies his chances against a small kid. A black person in leadership has to prove himself against every sniper who thinks he can do the job better. So when you think, and I hope you do, think about offering a prayer for people like Herman Ouseley and Bill Morris, because there are certain conditions attached to that which are peculiar. You get to recognise these tiresome situations when the guy is really saying, 'Why should you be promoted when I haven't been?' or 'Why should you, a foreigner, be issuing instructions to me in my own country?' You have to resist the temptation to get your retaliation in first!

Secondly, such black persons are subject to accusations of bias in favour of black people. The result is that if they are insecure in themselves they can bend over backwards too far to avoid appearing partial to black people or even too much at ease in pre-dominantly black situations. Personally, I lost those inhibitions many years ago when I first arrived in this country. Being anxious to be integrated, I went with the other clergy to Tom, the local barber. He had never cut a black person's hair before and hadn't a clue. He was apologetic but I insisted, although frankly the results of his efforts on my head were murderous to behold. It made me feel noble that I was suffering for a good cause. But every time I came through the door I could see his face fall. As a professional he knew he was not doing a good job, and so eventually, more out of compassion for him than anything else, I stopped going. Sometime later I discovered a black barber shop. The West Indian barber who was there was a guy who enjoyed hairdressing and had undertaken an expensive hairdresser's course – white people's hair of course. But after graduation he could not get a job in any white salon so he had to fall back on a black barber's. So here we were, two black people thrown together when both of us would have preferred an integrated setting.

From then on I have not worried about appearances, only to make sure that my actions would have been the same had the person been white. That is why the only priest to take me to an industrial tribunal accusing me of racial discrimination is black. Quite true. He was also the only black priest in my area at the time.

Next there are the relationships with the black community itself. Public office means public account-ability and the higher the office, the greater the accountability. It is galling for black people to see white officials play loose and fast with public funds to the benefit of their friends, but find that similarly placed black officials are not prepared to do the same to help them when their own needs are both real and great. But, however sympathetic the black official may be, however trying of his patience it may be to explain over and over again why he cannot follow the practices of his white counterparts, he must hold the line and not cut corners if he is to champion the cause of justice and black people without having constantly to be looking over his shoulder.

All this applies to me as a black bishop in the Church of England as it does to any black person in a high profile public post. But understandably such an appointment when, as was the case with me, it is the first of its kind, receives more than the usual amount of publicity and makes it difficult for one to take it in one's stride. So I was most grateful to the wise old priest, now dead, who was my spiritual adviser at the time. He urged me to see it as just an enlarged arena for the same service to the same God, who had been preparing me all the time for it. He had pointed out to me that few other bishops at the time of their appointment had had my experience of international politics such as chairing the World Council of Churches' Programme to Combat Racism. So much so that I had had discussions with both Joshua Nkomo and Robert Mugabe when they came to London for the pre-independence talks. Few had sat on a Royal Commission, few had established their credentials before appointment as campaigners for racial justice as I had, few had been so well-known from radio and television appearances. He himself had long been praying that I should be made a bishop and I was not to think that I was any less qualified than anyone else.

I think that I can say that in the almost 14 years that I have been a bishop, I have not consciously shirked when it fell to me to say what I believed to be true even though it was not popular, such as deploring the status accorded to Enoch Powell by having his body in Westminster Abbey overnight, or the recent bombing of Iraq. I would like to think that in my endeavour to care for God's people, encouraging them by word and example, and together with them witnessing to God's love of all Humankind, I have succeeded and failed in measure common to all bishops. I would like to think that I have kept reminding myself and reminding others that we cannot worship Jesus in church services and efficient organisations if we are also starving, jailing, raping and murdering Him in the persons of powerless human beings of any description. I know that I am not without friends and supporters, and I do not doubt that there are detractors. There is a long way yet to go and a great deal still to be done but I hope with God's help, not to drop the baton before I have reached the change-over point.

Ladies and gentlemen, friends, I don't know what you were expecting but that is what you got and I thank you very much for your patient hearing.

3
Marking the Black Anglican Celebration of the Decade of Evangelism

York Minster, UK, 24 July 1994

Genesis, chapter 45 verses 4-5
And Joseph said unto his brethren, Come near to me,
I pray you. And they came near. And he said,
I *am* Joseph your brother, whom ye sold into Egypt.
Now therefore be not grieved, nor angry with yourselves,
that ye sold me here hither:
for God did send me before you to preserve life.

Joseph was one of twelve brothers. Although eleven of them were older, bigger and stronger than he, he did not fear them because they were his brothers. So he told them of his dream which predicted that the time would come when they would all bow down to him. They responded by selling him into slavery in Egypt. *Joseph had faith in his brothers, and suffered because of it.*

In Egypt he became a dutiful and conscientious slave, and his master Potiphar was kind to him. In return, he loved his master. So when his master's wife issued him with a request/order that most young, healthy male servants would have obeyed with alacrity, he did not co-operate. But hell knows no fury like a woman scorned, so she had him thrown into prison. *Joseph had love for his master and suffered because of it.*

In prison he befriended other prisoners, encouraging them to have hope. In particular he supported the king's former butler, assuring him of his eventual restoration, and asking him, when he was restored to influence, to plead his [Joseph's] cause with the king. The butler was indeed eventually pardoned, but alas, he forgot all about Joseph, who was left to languish in prison. *Joseph had hope and suffered because of it.*

Joseph truly knew God, because of all the windows into God, none gives a clearer vision than that combination of virtue and suffering. I must have been very young indeed, when reading my way through the enormous large-print bible (with pictures) which dominated my grandmother's front room, I became captivated by the story of Joseph, and even today, many hard-bitten years later, I cannot read, or hear read, the account of Joseph making himself known to his brothers, without experiencing a tingling sensation. So perhaps it is not surprising that today I should want to share with you some thoughts occasioned by reflection on the story of Joseph – the suffering child of God who saved the lives of the brothers who had sold him into slavery. Because the faith, love and hope which God gave to Joseph, he has also given to us.

Many of us, who this weekend, are celebrating the presence and witness of Black Anglicans in Britain were born in British colonies. We were virtually born into the Church of England. For example, in Barbados, my birth certificate is useless as a legal document because it records only that a male child was born to my mother on a certain date. It was so taken for granted that every child would be baptised, that it is my baptismal certificate that is the legal document required by Government departments, because it is that which gives details of my full name, date of birth, parents' names and address etc. So with schools, churches, civil service, Army and Police all staffed by Christians, we were nurtured in societies that were overtly and unquestioningly Christian, and if it happened that those who wielded the power were all white, and were all from Britain, we had no reason to fear because we were all Christians. We were brothers. Like Joseph we had *faith* in our brothers.

There are many reasons that prompt people to move from the North of England to the South; from the provinces to the capital; from the rural districts to the cities. They make this migration with no sense of departing from their native country or culture. These same reasons brought many of us from the colonies to make our home in this country, and with an equally strong sense of our British birthright and Christian values. So whatever criticisms of this society we make, we make as sons and daughters within a family trying to help. When those whom we love and trust, try, like Potiphar's wife, to make wrong use of us, we will not co-operate, but like Joseph, we will continue to *love*.

Because Black Anglicans in Britain are only part of the wider black community, we live with the pain of a disproportionately high number of black people in prison and mental institutions, and very few in positions of status and influence in society as a whole; we bleed with the parents of Rolan Adams, Stephen Lawrence, Ruhullah Aramesh and the other young men whose lives were ended by murder for no reason other than that they were black. Even if the report of Parliament's Home Affairs Select Committee two months ago had not recorded that the seven and a half thousand racial incidents reported in 1992 were likely to be only one-sixteenth of the actual number, and that this number is growing, these facts would still be on our hearts because the suffering humanity they represent are part of us. So it is fitting that our deliberations this weekend will not only consider our place in mission, evangelism, church leadership, and the like, but will touch on health, housing, education and employment, criminal justice and racial harassment. It is fitting because we do believe that this country and culture are stronger for our presence here, and that the future for all our children – brown, black, white and double-ethnic, must be made better than the past. Like Joseph we have *hope*.

The hope that is in us derives from an unshakeable belief in the triumph of the good purposes of God. We are God's children, and we know that though ill-usage at the hands of others does cause us suffering, in the end such acts and such suffering are made to serve His good purpose. This is no pious hope because such a pattern is clearly seen in the lives of Joseph, of St Paul of countless others, and supremely in Our Lord and Saviour Jesus Christ. His death at the hands of those who wielded power in their time was but the precursor to the new life of His Resurrection which He now shares with those who are baptized in his name. For that reason we know that the pleasure and pain which are part of our human lot will pass with the passing of this earthly life, but true joy in the presence of God is everlasting, and it is *that* which is our destiny. It is this destiny which is foreshadowed in our *worship*, and accounts for its exuberance. Let the unperceptive sophisticate be embarrassed by this exuberance – an exuberance which incidentally still eludes even the most committed hand-raising charismatic! Let him think that this is mere opium for our suffering, or that we do not feel pain like other people! For our part we regard what we experience in our worship as an 'arabon' – a deposit which guarantees the full payment of ultimate reality. We are a black minority in a predominantly white church which itself is a white minority church in a predominantly Black Anglican

Communion! Confused? No need to be – our very existence is a prophetic sign, pointing to that heavenly assembly described in the Book of Revelation – a great multitude which no man could number, from all nations, and tribes and peoples and tongues.

Yet, although we rejoice to be who we are and to be where we are, there is no room for complacency for we know we are instruments of God's purpose. Some years ago I attended the opening of a new Benedictine priory, and heard the Abbot say: 'People ask me: "what will the monks do?"' and I reply: '"they are not here to *do* – they are here to *be*."' But I fear that this thought-provoking statement was quite lost on me because it immediately called to mind some irreverent graffiti which went like this: 'To do is to be – Sartre. To be is to do – Descartes. Do-be-do-be-do – Frank Sinatra!'

We know who we are in God's love. But this God who *calls* is also a God who sends, so we must ask what would He have us do, especially in this Decade of Evangelism?

First, the virtues of Faith, Love and Hope, like the colour of our skin, are gifts from God. And like all gifts from God they are not a reward for our merit, but equipments for service. So our *faith* in the Jesus who scandalised the respectable people of His day by His concern for the disabled, lepers, beggars and prostitutes, must show itself in active concern for those whose human dignity and personal worth are at risk today. Are you, through your church, caring for sickle cell anaemia or AIDs sufferers in your neighbourhood? Or for former mental hospital patients now located in the community? Or refugees and asylum seekers in your parish? If not, why not? And why wait for someone else to take the lead in this if, at the same time, you are asking for recognition of your own gifts in ministry and leadership?

Secondly, how best can we show our *love* for this nation of which we are a worthy part? The answer may surprise you – it is by prayer. We may not be privy to the inner workings of this society; we may not be frequent visitors to Downing Street or Chequers, be regularly consulted by Captains of Industry or briefed by MI5 and MI6. But we do not need to be. Because the substance of prayer is not *knowledge* – the substance of prayer is *love*, and thanks to the generosity of God, we have love in abundance.

And thirdly, *hope*; always there is hope. Even those of you who are younger than I am have seen great things in your lifetime. You have seen men walk on the moon. You have seen Nelson Mandela at the age of seventy vote for the first time in his life and become President of South Africa at the same time. This should not surprise us because these miracles are minor compared with the raising of Jesus from the dead. Yet God our Father did that. Why then should it be beyond our imagining that in our own lifetime, irrespective of the seeming invincibility of militarism and the arms industry in the present world order, we may yet see an end to war? – that peace, which is the fruit of justice, should take shape before our very eyes? Or that racism should end, and the one human *race* become the one human *family*?

Endowed by God's Holy Spirit with such faith, love and hope, we can, like Joseph, fall on our brothers' necks and say to them: 'Do not reproach yourselves for having sold us here for God sent us to preserve your lives. Our Father is still alive, and in this England's green and pleasant land, there is a building job to be done. Come, let us, together, get on with it.'

4
Southwark Diocese Race Relations Commission

Address to Southwark Diocesan Synod
St Bede's School, Redhill, Surrey, UK, 10 March 2001

St Matthew, chapter 7 verses 24-25
Therefore whosoever heareth these sayings of mine,
and doeth them, I will liken him unto a wise man,
which built his house upon a rock:
And the rain descended, and the floods came, and the
winds blew, and beat upon that house; and it fell not:
for it was founded upon a rock.

God is a Union of Absolute Power and Complete Goodness, entire within Godself, lacking nothing. Voluntarily choosing to give of Himself in creative activity, God brought into being a universe encompassing the mightiest planets and the minutest microbe. Somewhere within this range of multiform life, there is human life, and it is from within the limitations of this comparatively tiny feature of creation, that we human beings peer out at the rest of God's majestic creation.

Yet we Humankind dare to declare ourselves the *crown* of God's creation! Upon what basis is this self-importance founded? Why should life on Planet Earth be any more important than life on any other planet, whatever form that life may take? Is it because we are so important in our own eyes that we believe that God must concur with whatever status we choose to give ourselves? What is more, this self-importance going one step farther, some people have seen the scope there is for the arbitrary use of *power* in the management of human affairs, and have dispensed with the very concept of God! Remember the 'God is dead' theologians of the 1960s? And our power *is* arbitrary. For example a painting by Picasso is deemed to be worth thousands of pounds more than a painting by a three-year old from Croydon only because we say that it is. Similarly, millions go barefoot in Africa while a single person elsewhere owns more than a thousand pairs of shoes because we choose to let it be that way. It is this combination of power, arbitrary judgement, and self-importance that has given the world anti-semitism, slavery, colonialism, Nazism, apartheid and segregation.

We Christians also hold a high appreciation of humanity yet we avoid the excesses of such self-importance, because we do so for a very different reason. Whether we are shamefaced about it or not when we debate with academics and intellectuals, we must claim *revelation and faith* as the high ground on which we take our stand, and assert that a hallmark of God's relations with His world is *particularity*. Particularity is not the same as favouritism. *God does choose people and things, but to be chosen by God is not to denote superiority over those not similarly chosen, but a particularity of all such who are equally precious in His eyes.* Our high claim for humanity, is that God chose to share in the life of *all* His creation by becoming human in a *particular* person, a man named Jesus from the village of Nazareth, who was born in Bethlehem 2000 years ago. This choice did not mean that Nazareth was more precious than *all* other villages; Bethlehem the greatest of all towns; Jewish people more dear than any other nation; men worth more than women; or brown-skinned people more precious in God's eyes than black-skinned, pink-skinned and yellow-skinned people! What it does mean is that the presence of God in the particularity of Jesus signifies that God is present in every village, in every town, in every nationality, in each gender, in persons of every hue, all of which and all of whom are equally precious in his sight.

That is the bedrock of Christian belief, and it is that rock on which every construction for proper human relations must be built. *Human* relations, note, not 'race' relations, because there is only one race – the human race – and it should be humbling to remember that that one and the same race has produced Adolf Hitler and Nelson Mandela; Idi Amin and Albert Schweitzer. Whatever immediate or short-term emphases may be made necessary by events at specific times and in specific places, such emphases must never be allowed to do injury to the fundamental truth that every human being is made in the image of God; is someone for whom Christ died, and whose *true* worth can neither be enhanced nor diminished by nationality, ethnic origin, gender or colour.

Since the Church of Christ is called to act out its prophetic role in society by ordering its own life in a way which would be a model for all human communities, it can never rest content with a situation in which life in this Church of one faith, one baptism, one Lord is a mere mirror-image of life in society. In society a person's place of birth, ethnic group and even accent are more definitive of that person's value than her or his humanity. We have only to examine the manner and language of the current debate about asylum seekers to see that this is so. So the World Council of Churches, in its struggle to proclaim the Gospel in the 1960s and 1970s, called on its member-churches to focus on Liberation Theology and the struggle for freedom by oppressed peoples; the human and land rights of aboriginal and native peoples; and white racism, in a world ordered by power, self-interest and arbitrary judgement. It is to the credit of our Southwark diocese, that against mainstream Church of England, which at best was sluggish and at worst downright hostile to such a call, we tried to respond and eventually established the Southwark Diocese Race Relations Commission. True, some pretty awful things had been happening on our doorstep. There has been the shooting of Cherry Groce in her own home by Police in Brixton; the still unsolved deaths of thirteen young black people in a fire in New Cross; the Brixton disturbances in which a plain clothes police-man was photographed by a Sunday newspaper wielding a pickaxe handle, and the Police assured me that I was the only person to complain about it; the black Sunday School teacher at my local church of St John's East Dulwich who was so badly assaulted by Police that they had to award her £26,000 damages. But even in Southwark Diocese not every one was friendly; the Commission staggered through the 1980s but did not survive the 1990s.

We who have shared in the leadership of the Commission over the years offer no apology for the emphases we chose. We had no interest in recruiting black people for photo-opportunities and superficial talk of reconciliation in a Church where far too many people still believed that the plight of black people had nothing to do with them, and shared the prevailing political sentiments that Britain was being swamped by such people. Some of us were veterans who knew that institutional racism in the Police and other important institutions in our society did not begin when Judge McPherson chose to admit that it existed. It was what we lived with in Church and Society day in and day out. We also knew at first hand the alienation of young black people who were embarrassed, and sometimes angered by the daily humiliation of their parents by people who wielded power in this Society and wielded it arbitrarily, judging them on the basis of their colour, accents, and nationality. Rather, our task was to help these young people to value themselves without devaluing others. Hence the annual residential weekends open to all young people in the diocese, black and white alike. Nor were we interested in confrontational engagements to establish our radical credentials. Long before the name Stephen Lawrence meant anything to many people outside the Black Community, his parents had enlisted the help of the Commission's director David Udo, as the only person to speak for them. There are those among us who despise weakness, and mistook David's gentleness for weakness. Such persons know the price of everything and the value of nothing.

The prophet Martin Luther King Jnr in his last speech before his assassination on 4 April 1968, uttered these words: '… God has allowed me to go up to the mountain. And I have looked over, and I have seen the Promised Land. I may not get there with you, but I want you to know tonight, that we, as a people, will get to the Promised Land …'

That was some thirty-three years ago, so under-standably there are those among us who may never have heard King in his lifetime, and who know neither the words nor tune of 'We shall overcome'. It may be that in these days of the internet and the mobile telephone we will never again march the streets with arms linked in a visible demonstration of common humanity and God's equal love for all His children. The Southwark Diocese Race Relations Commission dies, and the Minority Ethnic Anglican Concerns Committee is born. Different time, different emphases. But let it be the same journey with the same goal of the same Promised Land – that of a British Society infected with the Christian principles of human worth, love and justice, at peace and at ease with itself, because in the diocese of Southwark at least it has been demonstrated that this is possible. For this to happen, we must rely, not on a Committee, not on a Code, not on a Principle, not on a Book, though these all have their place, but on a *Person* now alive, but who suffered and died for these ideals, Jesus the Incarnate Son of the Almighty Creator. No storms or floods can destroy a house built on *that* rock.

5

Address to Mark the International Day for the Remembrance of the Slave Trade and its Abolition

Merseyside Maritime Museum, Albert Dock, Liverpool, UK
23 August 2001

Mr Mayor of Liverpool, My Lord Bishop, Baroness Howells, Your Worships, Ladies and Gentlemen. Why a Remembrance of the Slave Trade and its Abolition? As more and more weapons of mass destruction become available to more and more people, the search for peaceful co-existence among the peoples of this shrinking planet becomes ever more urgent. Feelings of superiority, inferiority and resentment can shade into aggression and violence, and this threatens the only basis there is for peaceful co-existence, namely a mutual respect in which we see everyone else as our equal. Without this there is no hope for any of us. It is therefore imperative that we identify whatever might give rise to mistaken ideas of superiority and inferiority in order to destroy its poison. This is one very good reason for a Remembrance of the Slave Trade and its Abolition.

Centuries ago, there were, here in Europe, many nations with varying systems of government, and made up of farmers, craftsmen, artists, musicians, priests, soldiers, teachers, kings and queens, who were husbands and wives, daughters and sons, nephews, nieces, grandparents and grandchildren. They were human.

It was not a case of 'nations' in Europe and 'tribes' in Africa. Both could be described as either nations or tribes.

But Europeans travelled to Africa, violently assaulted the Africans in their own home, shackled them in leg-irons, and transported them in insanitary conditions of disease and malnutrition, thousands of miles across the sea to the Caribbean and the Americas.

There they sold them by auction to other Europeans for whom they had to work without payment on sugar and cotton plantations and at any task or in any conditions inflicted on them. The Africans who rebelled against this treatment were beaten, mutilated and sometimes killed. Rebellions were put down with the utmost savagery, while European plantation-owners became richer and richer from the unpaid labour of Africans.

It is important that the descendants of those Africans and the descendants of those Europeans both know that the difference between their forbears was not in intelligence, or ability, or in courage, but that Europeans had guns and the Africans did not. Once this is recognized, today's Afro-Britons, Euro-Britons, double-ethnic Britons and all other Britons can be true to themselves as equal Britons. And of course we know that 'Britons never, never, never shall be slaves!' That is the second very good reason for the Remembrance of the Slave Trade and its Abolition.

The primary driving force behind European dehumanising of Africans was the acquisition of wealth. There was money to be made from buying and selling Africans and from their unpaid labour – wealth for individuals and families in Britain, cities in Britain and the economy in Britain. Years later, this is what Sir Winston Churchill had to say:

> The West Indies, 200 years ago, bulked very largely in the minds of all people who were making Britain and the British Empire. Our possession of the West Indies, like that of India – the colonial plantation and development as they were then called – gave us the strength, but especially the capital, the wealth at a time when no European nation possessed such a reserve, which enabled us, not only to acquire this world-wide appendage of possessions which we have, but also to lay the foundations of the commercial and financial leadership, which, when the world was young, when everything outside Europe was undeveloped, enabled us to make our great position in the world.

Wealth is generated by a combination of capital and labour. Those who contributed the capital centuries ago were allowed by wills and legacies to transmit the profits from their capital to their descendants in later generations; those who contributed the labour were not able to provide for their descendants in the same way. But the latter have as much right to the benefits of life in Britain today as do the former. Everyone living in Britain today needs to be informed and reminded of this fact. And this is a third very good reason for the Remembrance of the Slave Trade and its Abolition.

For years the proper relationship between Africans and Europeans has been distorted by the imperialism of language. Europeans, whose skin-colour is nearer to pink than white, nonetheless appropriated the term white for self-description. 'White' is associated with purity, cleanliness, light and truth, while 'black' is everything that white is not. Today we are seeing the emergence of another imperialism – a new phenomenon which can be described as 'cultural imperialism', aided and abetted by Hollywood. Native Americans had welcomed the Mayflower Pilgrims and other European asylum seekers, and shown them how to survive and thrive in a strange land. But Hollywood fed us a diet of movies in which so-called 'Red Indians' are portrayed as savage killers whose only aim in life was to scalp the brave white pioneers. This process is now being applied to other episodes of history, and soon the Hollywood version of any event will replace the factual in the consciousness of generations who read less than they view. Recent films on subjects such as the sinking of the Titanic and the code-breaking Enigma are pointers in this direction. It may be that one day some Hollywood producer may decide that there is money to be made with a film which shows that Africans were so keen to get to the good life of the Caribbean and America that they pleaded with the ship owners to take them there! Never mind the truth – give the Public what they want! We must guard against this cavalier treatment of truth. This is a fourth very good reason for a Remembrance of the Slave Trade and its Abolition.

Although Africans had always resisted their enslavement and their rebellions were making the plantations less profitable and increasingly unmanageable, there was still great opposition in Britain to any change. However in 1793 a small but determined group mounted a campaign for the abolition of slavery and the slave trade. At the heart of this movement were a group of Christians gathered around the Rev'd Jon Venner, Rector of Holy Trinity, Clapham and included persons prominent in public life such as Wilberforce, Clarkson, Sharpe, Buxton, Thornton, Stephen, Macauley and others. They drew upon evidence and experiences supplied by a remarkable African who had himself been sold into slavery, Olaudah Equiano, and eventually their efforts were rewarded when the British Parliament outlawed the Slave Trade in 1807 and Slavery in 1833. A sad note in all this was that whereas compensation of more than a million pounds was paid to plantation owners for the loss of their slaves, nothing was paid to the survivors of the twenty million Africans who had been enslaved by them. Great changes can be brought about by small beginnings when a cause is just. That is a fifth very good reason for the Remembrance of the Slave Trade and its Abolition.

Christians should be the first to recognise that 'all men are created equal, and endowed by their Creator with certain inalienable rights, among which are life, liberty and the pursuit of happiness.' We of the twenty-first century need to be reminded that Christ expects more of us than church maintenance, ecclesiastical infighting and debates over the ordination of women. If we are to help men and women to live as God intends, then no matter how strong and powerful may be the forces that are dehumanising God's children, we must engage with such forces – be they Slave Trade, Arms Trade, Racism or the odious practice of ethnic-clearing. Note that I say Ethnic Clearing and not ethnic-*cleansing*. It is bad enough to clear people out of their homes and countries without also implying that they are vermin! For a Christian, if a practice is morally wrong and theologically wrong, it cannot be politically right. And this is a sixth very good reason for the Remembrance of the Slave Trade and its Abolition.

A paradox of this despicable epoch of human history is that it has also been the occasion for an almost superhuman act of forgiveness. The rape and pillage of Africa have not been followed by any vengeful atrocities by Africans against vulnerable Europeans. On the contrary, the recent peaceful transition from apartheid South Africa to democratic South Africa is but a *particular* example of a *general* African generosity and forgiveness. Similarly, the modern Caribbean is a microcosm of what the world could be like, where, in the aftermath of slavery and colonialism, people of every ethnic group – African, Asian, Creole, European, Oriental – can have the freedom to be who they are. That is a seventh good reason for the Remembrance of the Slave Trade and its Abolition.

Finally, Ladies and Gentlemen, I believe I speak for us all in thanking the Trustees and Staff of the National Museum and Galleries on Merseyside for staging this event; in congratulating them on its success, and in wishing them even greater success for similar imaginative and visionary projects in the future. I would like also to thank them for inviting me to share it with you. Thank you for your patient hearing.

6
Japheth 'Jeff' Ebenezer Crawford of Barbados

who died in Britain on 25 December 2003
Thanksgiving Service for his life
St Luke's Church, Brighton, St George, Barbados
13 March 2004

Galatians, chapter 6 verse 10
As we have therefore opportunity,
let us do good unto all ...

It is fitting that at services such as this, there is both a eulogy and a sermon. The eulogy is meant to remind us of the person who has died, of the circumstances in which he lived, and influences which shaped his life. Ralph Straker's eulogy has been most helpful in reminding some of us and informing others of our late brother's life and activities in Britain.

The sermon, on the other hand, is meant to remind all who hear, of the eternal truths. That we are not in this world by accident, but that we have been created by a God of Love who has a purpose for our lives; that the time will come when each of us will be called from this life, and that there is a life beyond the grave. We know this because Our Lord Jesus was raised from the grave and He said of Himself, *I* am the Resurrection and I am life. In other words it is through Him that we pass from this life to new life.

So the sermon is not a second eulogy, but even so it will happen that it will touch on the witness of the departed, in this case our brother Jeff Crawford.

Five hundred and ninety-seven years before the birth

of Jesus, Jerusalem was captured and occupied by the Babylonians. The Babylonians took all the leading people in Jerusalem, as well as the craftsmen and the soldiers, and any who might lead rebellion against the occupiers, to live in Babylon. Naturally these captives hoped that it would not be long before they could return home and many of them were inclined to sit down by the rivers of Babylon and weep for home. They were not to know that this Exile would last for more than sixty years and that it would be their children and grandchildren, born in Babylon and equipped with the most modern skills, education and sophistication, who would one day enrich the land of their forebears. In the meantime it fell to God's prophet, Jeremiah, to tell them what they did not want to hear, namely: 'Settle down in the new country, look after your families and play a full part in the life of the country in which you find yourselves.' As a result Jeremiah was not popular, and his name has come down to us as the name for a dismal prophet. But such is the fate of those who must speak the unpalatable truth in the name of God.

The story of the Jewish Exile is only analogous to the Caribbean migration to Britain of the 1950s and 1960s, not an exact precedent. But people who had grown up in the Caribbean proud to be British and proud to be Christian, were shocked by the un-British lack of welcome, and the un-Christian lack of fellowship they encountered, when they were invited to Britain to work in hospitals, transport, etc. Many felt trapped because what they wanted more than anything was to get back to the Caribbean, but for various reasons they could not. For the most part they had been conditioned by their upbringing in the Caribbean to respect those in authority such as employers, teachers and police officers and not to question their actions. They had also been taught to go to Church, say their prayers and leave every-thing in God's hands. So their reaction to this hurtful experience was to make the best of a bad job even when things were getting worse rather than better. Just as one of the prophets God had raised up for the Jewish migrants in their time of need was Jeremiah; so one of the prophets God raised up for the Caribbean migrants in our time of need was Jeff Crawford.

You have heard in Ralph Straker's eulogy about some of the things Jeff did. I can attest to these because I was involved in some of them. For example, he invited me to be the main speaker at the launch of the Caribbean Teachers Association; I have in my scrapbook a Guardian Newspaper photograph in March 1968 which shows him and me on a bitterly cold day, with placards outside London Transport's headquarters, demanding that they end the racial discrimination against black drivers and conductors who applied to be inspectors. And month after month he was in his place as Secretary at meetings of the Standing Conference of West Indian Organisations. Standing Conference exposed to the wider public the Police mistreatment of Caribbean and other black people which was commonplace. In addition, I gave four lectures to over 1,000 policemen in West London – not greatly appreciated by them at the time. Jeff knew the importance of this issue for the community and he stayed with it. He was regularly in confrontation with police spokespersons on radio and television, always with patience and good humour. He was not against the Police – only against the things they were doing. But for the Police he was Public Enemy No. 1. In later years they came to appreciate his true worth, and when he was appointed by the Government to the Police Complaints Authority, he was scrupulously fair in his oversight of investigations into Police misconduct. It was no surprise that the Metropolitan

Police provided a twelve person Guard of Honour at his funeral, and their representatives spoke of him in glowing terms.

Those were *some* of the things Jeff *did*. Equally important was the *way he did them*. Because he was never on the make or on the take, he could not be corrupted. I remember hearing many attacks on him, but I cannot remember ever hearing him defend himself. He was a patient listener and encourager. His address book was elastic, and right up to his death, he could always tell you who were the most likely persons or the persons best equipped to help with a particular piece of community service, giving you their phone numbers and addresses on the spot. He was envious of no one, and although I cannot prove this, I strongly suspect that he declined inclusion on the Honours List. But we can say of him as was said of Abraham Lincoln: 'Now he belongs to the Ages.'

In some burial places you sometimes find at the head of the grave, instead of a cross, a broken-off pillar. This is not a Christian symbol but a borrowing from Greek thought – suggesting that the person had died before his time. But we Christians believe that our time is in God's hands, as are all the Times and Ages, and He sees to it that we all have time sufficient to do what He wants us to do. Early death is no more a sign of God's displeasure than long life a sign of His approval. Far more important is what we do with the time He has given us. St Paul's advice to the Galatians is short and to the point: *While we have time, let us do good to all.* He does not say do good to those who do good to us, or those who will be grateful to us, or those who are our nearest and dearest, but to *all*. The passing of a great servant of the community is an occasion for each of us to consider the contribution we are making or should be making to the community in which we are living.

Nowadays we do not need much encourage-ment to live selfish lives. It is easily done because most of us no longer need to wonder where our next meal is coming from, and we can spend as much time as we like doing whatever takes our fancy. We may know that there are serious needs in the community but we can convince ourselves that Government should pay some-one to meet them. But thank God we are not all like that. Some people make a point of being good neighbours; they keep an eye on elderly people who live on their own; they provide transport for disabled people for whom a period of browsing the shelves of a supermarket keeps them happy for a week; they encourage neighbourhood children to study by offering a money prize for every CXC certificate they obtain:[1] they telephone recently bereaved people to offer sympathy. And in church on Sundays they remember by name, in their silent prayers, the people they know to be in need. There can never be too many such people, and if you are not one of them; now is the time to become one of them. To make that decision now, here at this service, would be a tribute to Jeff's life and work.

And it would be more than that. You will remember that when Jesus told a young man that all God wanted him to do was to love God completely and to love his neighbour as himself, the young man asked Jesus who was his neighbour. In reply Jesus told him the story we call the Parable of the Good Samaritan, which showed that neighbourliness has nothing to do with race, colour or creed, gender or nationality. It has everything to do with rendering assistance to those who need it whoever they may be. What Jesus said to that young man then, He is saying to us now. If we have ears to hear, let us hear, and while we have time, let us do good to all.

7
Rudy Narayan of Guyana
Funeral Service
St Matthew's Church, Brixton, London, UK, 10 July 1998

The lectionary which some clergy and others use for their daily Bible readings, recommends for today's reading, a passage from St Matthew's Gospel, chapter 10 beginning at verse 26. In this passage Jesus is telling His followers what life will be like when they speak in His name, and giving them some advice. This chapter includes the following words from Jesus: *So do not be afraid of them. There is nothing concealed that will not be disclosed, or hidden that will not be made known. What I tell you in the dark, speak in the daylight, what is whispered in your ear, proclaim from the housetops. Do not fear those who kill the body but cannot destroy the soul ...*

Whether Rudy was deliberately following the advice of Jesus as a conscious act of faith, I do not know. But certainly his work was characterised by the kind of fearlessness and forthright speaking in the cause of justice which Jesus asked of His followers, and it may be no coincidence that even as today we are giving thanks to God for Rudy's life and commending his soul to his Maker, people around the world are reading those words and finding strength to speak out for what they know is right, irrespective of the cost to themselves.

Yesterday, in Westminster Abbey, a number of us were present for the unveiling and dedication of ten statues commemorating Christian martyrs of this century, some of who paid the ultimate price for this stand against injustice. A highlight of that service was the reading of some words from Archbishop Romero in an interview two weeks before he was murdered in his cathedral in El Salvador. He said:

> I have frequently been threatened with death. I ought to say that as a Christian, I do not believe in death without resurrection. If they kill me I will rise again in the people of El Salvador. I am not boasting. I say it with the greatest humility.
>
> I am bound, as a pastor, by a divine command, to give my life for those who I love, and that is, all Salvadorians, even those who are going to kill me. If they manage to carry out their threats from this moment I offer my blood for the redemption and resurrection of El Salvador.
>
> Martyrdom is a grace from God which I do not believe I deserve. But if God accepts the sacrifice of my life, then may my blood be the seed of liberty, and a sign that hope will soon become a reality.
>
> May my death, if it is accepted by God, be for the liberation of my people, and as a witness of hope in what is to come. Can you tell them, if they succeed in killing me, that I pardon and bless those who do it. But I wish that they could realise that they are wasting their time. A bishop may die, but the Church of God, which is the people, will never die.

Truth and justice are of God and although all who suffer for the stand they take may not pay the ultimate price or die in dramatic circumstances, their suffering is not unknown to God or their offering unacceptable to Him. All of us can only witness where He places us. No-one who knew Rudy can deny that he was abundantly talented, with just the kinds of gifts which are most useful to those people whose greatest concern is to promote themselves. He was personable, charming, eloquent, humorous and highly intelligent. But he chose to use these gifts, not for himself, but to help the cause of justice for those who were being denied the rights to which they were entitled. Such determination should have made him a hero to those who shared his profession – instead they chose to brand him as a trouble-maker, someone who rocked the boat. And yet you have only to consider some of the revelations emerging in the current Stephen Lawrence murder investigation inquiry to recognise the reality of the evils he was fighting. But if only a few of those whose better chances have come their way because of his fearless challenges to unjust practices, inherit but a little of his spirit, he will have made a significant contribution.

An occasion such as this when we come to say farewell to someone we knew well, should be an occasion for all of us to take stock of our own lives. By what do we measure the purpose of our own existence? Why should we be healthy, comfortable and well-fed in a world where so many are not? Is this meant to be so? Are we more deserving of God's love than the people of the Sudan who are dying of starvation before our eyes on television? Or do these situations exist because the gifts God has given to us to right these wrongs, we choose instead to use for our own self-promotion? It that is so, then it is sin – falling below the standards to which God calls us.

We may never know how successful Rudy Narayan and others like him were in their efforts to make the world a better place. Only God knows that. What we do know is that they tried, anyway. May they rest in Christ and rise with Him in glory, and may God grant us, in our time, courage to try also.

8

Cecil George Collier of Jamaica

Thanksgiving Service for his life
St James's Church, Piccadilly, London, UK
17 September 1994

1 John, chapter 3 verse 14
We know that we have passed from death unto life,
because we love the brethren...

I would like to begin with Leigh Hunt's poem 'Abou Ben Adhem.'

> Abou Ben Adhem (may his tribe increase!)
> Awoke one night from a deep dream of peace,
> And saw, within the moonlight in his room,
> Making it rich, and like a lily in bloom,
> An angel writing in a book of gold: –
> Exceeding peace had made Ben Adhem bold,
> And to the presence in the room he said,
> 'What writest thou?' – The vision raised its head,
> And with a look made of all sweet accord,
> Answered, 'The names of those who love the Lord.'
> 'And is mine one?' said Abou. 'Nay, not so,'
> Replied the angel. Abou spoke more low,
> But cheerly still; and said, 'I pray thee, then,
> Write me as one that loves his fellow-men.'
>
> The angel wrote, and vanished. The next night
> It came again with a great wakening light,
> And show'd the names whom love of God had blest,
> And lo! Ben Adhem's name led all the rest.

Like Abou Ben Adhem, Cecil Collier showed his love for God by demonstrating his love for his brothers and sisters. Consciously or unconsciously he reflected the words of the Apostle in 1 John, chapter 4 verses 20-21: *But if a man says, I love God, while hating his brother, he is a liar. If he does not love the brother who he has seen, it cannot be that he loves God whom he has not seen.* And the Apostle James in his epistle, chapter 2 verses 14-17 says: *Suppose a brother or a sister is in rags with not enough food for the day, and one of you says: Good luck to you, keep yourselves warm and have plenty to eat but does nothing to supply their bodily needs, what is the good of that? So is faith; if it does not lead to action, it is in itself a lifeless thing.*

Cecil Collier was essentially an *action* man. I last saw him in Jamaica five years ago, but my earliest encounters with him were in the early 1960s in this country. At that time the prevalent view among the public figures who presented themselves as friends of the West Indian community was that unlike other immigrants West Indians were English speaking and shared the same cultural values as local English people. In their view there was no need for separate black or West Indian organisations, but instead the way to integration was for West Indians to join the existing political and social organisations.

But even before the dockers marched or Enoch Powell achieved notoriety, Cecil was one of the few who recognised the difference between 'integration' and 'assimilation' and while working for the former rejected the latter. He saw that there was a real gap between the rhetoric and the reality, and what was needed was not advice to West Indians on how to suffer silently, but action to ease or prevent such suffering. He saw that if black people were to take their place equally alongside everyone else in this country in political, educational, social and every other sphere of decision-making, we had to question the systems and offer our own solutions to the problems we faced. He was not content to follow leaders blindly, and he saw that is was those ordinary West Indians slaving away on the lowest rungs of the employment ladder in London Transport and British Rail, National Health Service hospital kitchens and cleaning rooms, factory canteens etc. who would be the bedrock of whatever black community would emerge from this country. Self-help, with initiative and leadership coming from such ranks would have to be the way forward for West Indians. So even while he was furthering his own studies and earning his living by working with the then London County Council, he found time to help found, and lead, the Geneva and Summerleyton Community Association in Brixton; to do what he could through the West Indian Standing Conference, and wherever possible to make representations on behalf of West Indians in this country. Later, when he was recruited to serve as a Counsellor with the Jamaica High Commission in London, he was able to inform the leadership of that Commission, and even the Government back in Jamaica, of the real bread-and-butter issues facing Jamaicans in this country and inform them in the way that Jamaicans saw them. It never occurred to him that he was serving the community at any cost to himself, because he identified so closely with the community that for him any community gain was his own personal gain.

It is more appropriate that it is in *worship* that we are assembled today to remember Cecil and to give thanks for his life. Because we would want young black people in Britain today to adopt for themselves Cecil's ideals of community service. We would want them to know that he was nurtured in a culture which rendered to

God His rightful place as the Father of us all and Giver of all good things. We would want them to know that even if their contemporaries in this country prefer to believe that they have no need for God, it must not be so among them. For we know that it is the same God who was with our forefathers in Jamaica and elsewhere who sustained them in their journey to this country and aided their survival; that God revealed to us in Jesus Christ as a God of love, who will surely be our own Guide and Protector in future troublous times.

It is to this God that we return thanks for the life and companionship of our departed brother, Cecil; this God who will stand by his widow Ariadne – herself an outstanding servant of the community over the years in this country, in the USA and in Jamaica – and the other members of Cecil's family in their bereavement, and into whose loving arms we now commend his soul. To this living, loving God, be ascribed, as is most justly due, all honour and glory, praise and thanksgiving, now and forever. Amen.

SECTION TWO

CALLED TO SERVE

9
The Ordination of Twenty-One Women Deacons to the Priesthood

Southwark Cathedral, UK, 21 May 1994

Jeremiah, chapter 1 verse 5
Before I formed thee in the belly I knew thee; and before thou camest forth out of the womb I sanctified thee...
Jeremiah, chapter 31 verse 3
...I have loved thee with an everlasting love...

This world, before or since, has never known a division in human society greater than that which existed between Jew and non-Jew at the time the Church was born. That was a chasm wider than apartheid's division between black and white; Middle East division between Israeli and Palestinian; cold war division between capitalist and communist, and *within* these divisions, and *in addition* to them the division between male and female. When the Council of the Apostles in Jerusalem (recorded in Acts, chapter 15) rescued the Church from the fate of being just another Jewish sect destined for extinction, by ruling that in giving his Holy Spirit God made no distinction between Jew and non-Jew, this wonderful act of worship in which we are today engaged became an inevitability.

The cultural subordination of women which has crippled the Church for so many centuries, however substantial, however widespread and however traditional could not withstand forever the consuming fire of the Holy Spirit. It says something about God's love for the world of Humankind, not only for his Church – that other events up to now visible only to the eye of faith – such as the end of apartheid, and the prospect of a Palestinian Homeland – virtually coincide with today's small step for woman, today's giant step for Humankind. But what was *not* inevitable was that you and I should have lived to see it.

In certain large buildings with many rooms and long corridors, such as hospitals, municipal offices etc, different coloured lines on the floor lead to specific points, or sometimes there is a light overhead which you are asked to follow. Each of you ordinands here this morning has been following your own coloured line from birth, and what a kaleidoscope of experiences – of joys and sorrows, anxieties and relief, losses and gains, sacrifices and unexpected gifts, regrets and delightful surprises – these have been made as they crossed and criss-crossed relationships, epochs, events, even continents to bring you here to this place and to this moment. I know this, for some of you have graciously taken me into your confidence and shared much with me. Some good you must have all done – some wrong also; some evil you may have endured; wittingly or unwittingly you may have contributed to other people's disasters. There will surely be things in your past of which you are very proud, and others of which you are heartily ashamed. Only God – certainly neither you nor I – knows which outweighs the other, and where the balance lies. So we all have good cause to be thankful that your presence here this morning is not a result of your own merit or achievement, your virtue or your cunning. It is in no way a compensation for your suffering, or reward for your faith, patience, perseverance or good works. It is not even dependent upon that mythical male invention – 'woman's intuition!'

Shelagh, Clare, Hilary, Sara, Val, Barbara, Barbara, Barbara, Barbara, Sally, Sylvia, Angela, Frances, Julia, Marian, Gillian, Dawn, Mary, Mary, Audrey and Gaynor, let me ask each of you to recall the *year* in which you were born; now the *month* in which you were born; now the *date* on which you were born. On that same day around the world there were thousands of babies born. Three out of every five of those children died before reaching the age of five, and no doubt others since then. That *you* should be among the tiny number of survivors is in no way a result of your own doing.

So, why is it that you are here to be ordained priest in the Church of God? It is for one reason, and one reason only. And it is this: *That God looked on you, and loved you, and wanted you to be a priest in the Church and has seen to it that you become one.* Thanks be to God! From first to last it is God's graciousness, generosity and love so aptly described in Jeremiah, chapter 1 verse 1 *Before I formed you in the womb, I knew you, before you were born, I consecrated you*, and Jeremiah, chapter 31 verse 3 *I have loved you with an everlasting love, so I am constant in my affection for you.* So there can be no doubt that your call is real. It is a call to replicate in your own circumstances the same wish to glorify God by your own life at all times, public and private; the same obedience to God's will, the same selfless concern for God's vulnerable children, to which Jesus Himself was called. What is *not* inevitable is your own acceptance of, or faithfulness to, such a call.

Christ was once approached by a young man who wanted to follow Him. And Christ looked on him and loved him. Then Christ told him: 'One thing you lack – detach yourself from your present wealth and status and come with Me.' At that the young man went away sadly. Jesus had every sympathy with the young man.

He knew what He was asking was difficult, but He asked it nonetheless. Today Jesus challenges *you* in the same way, and you too have a choice. After this service, will you also, in heart and mind go away? We pray not. Rather we pray that just trying to be like Jesus you will each have a fruitful and fulfilling ministry.

For Jesus is giving *you* a share in *His* priestly ministry. A priest is a person who presides at the offering of sacrifice, and because in Christ, Priest and Victim are one and the same, there is, in this ministry to which you are being called a mingling of suffering and power. You are human as Jesus was, and you will shrink from suffering as He did. You and I do not doubt that Jesus on the cross could have called on the unseen hosts to come to His assistance, or stepped down from the cross and walked away. That power was always there, but such power when used for self-protection is empty of *love*. Do not covet such power. On the other hand, the strength that there is in love comes from *suffering* – that is why the analogy of childbirth is so apt – with childbirth suffering is vindicated by the joy of creating a living object and vehicle of love. Some of you will have known that kind of suffering and that kind of joy at first hand; others will have known the even greater pain of utter loneliness and betrayal, and then the joy of being loved. So not for you the empty triumphalism of persons who have vanquished adversaries or outwitted opponents to capture a prize that was being withheld; but instead that godly fear as the enormity of Christ's love for you and his confidence in you, dawns upon you. How will you fare? Will the eternal destiny of some poor soul be affected by the quality of your priestly ministrations on her deathbed? Will some wrongdoer be confirmed in his wrongdoing because he sees in you a fellow-offender untroubled by a guilty conscience? Sadly, I know of a priest who once declined to answer a summons to the bedside of a dying parishioner because it was his day off and he was preparing for a supper party. I pray that that is not how you learned Christ. For that is not worthy of the world from sin, and who has assigned to you a unique share in His own world-redeeming and world-sanctifying ministry.

The unfolding of this ministry continues, and just as the moment of the Incarnation once hung upon the decision of a simple village girl named Mary, so we are not to know what stupendous and earth-shaking events may yet be dependent upon some common-place action of a devout priest who happens to be you. Archbishop Desmond Tutu traces the first stirrings of his call to the priesthood to the sight of a white priest in apartheid-ridden South Africa, removing his hat in deference to a black domestic servant – his mother. That priest was young Trevor Huddleston whose faithfulness to Christ has played no small part in winning many souls for Christ, and the liberty of generations yet unborn. Such can be the power of faithfulness to the Christ who first loved us!

Two final thoughts. First, none of you is being ordained against your will, so it will be out of place for you now to say 'yes' to a call from Christ to suffer with Him, only in later years to be envious of con-temporaries who have found happiness in material wealth and popular acclaim. Christ gives no promise of such fulfilment. Secondly, you are not being ordained in a vacuum. You are being ordained into the Sacred Ministry of Christ's Holy, Catholic and Apostolic Church. The Church of God may not be perfect – how could it be when it comprises fallible human beings – but it is the instrument Christ has chosen to make Himself known to every new generation. Beware the temptation to try your hand at forging a better instrument as though the Church is meant to be an End in itself and our task is to achieve its perfection! The Church is part of God's purpose for His world, and because He loves us, He has assigned to each of us a part in this purpose. It should be enough for us to trust Him and to play our part. And it may be, that just as we have lived to see *this* day, we shall live to see the day when the one human *race* becomes the one human *family* and hear Christ's cry from the cross become a full-throated roar of triumph: 'Tetelestai – it is completed!'

10
Confirmation Sermon

Croydon Episcopal Area, UK, March 1992

At the outset, let me ask you to memorise two verses from St John's Gospel, and after this service, find them in your bible and underline them. Then, in your own prayer book, write them out in full with today's date to remind you of your Confirmation, and to remind you also, whenever you feel put down by other people, or whenever you are tempted to let yourself down by some unworthy action, who you are, and how highly Jesus thinks of you. The verses are:

St John, chapter 15 verses 12-14
This is my commandment,
That ye love one another, as I have loved you.
Greater love hath no man than this,
that a man lay down his life for his friends.
Ye are my friends...

Since no one can force anyone to love against his or her own will, this seems at first sight, a strange thing for Jesus to say. But here he is speaking to people who believe in God and who accept that they should live their lives according to God's commandments. Until then they had thought of God's commandments as the Ten Commandments recorded in the Bible in Exodus, chapter 20. Because in these days, sadly, there are many people who know *of* the commandments but do not know what they are I am tempted to read them out! I will not do so but I ask you to look them up in Exodus 20.

By using the word 'commandments' Jesus makes it clear that He is speaking with the authority of God. He also makes it clear that love is the right relationship between those who *believe* in God. The Ten Commandments can be summed up in the short statement, 'you shall *love* the Lord your God will all your heart, with all your mind, with all your soul, and with all your strength, and you shall *love* your neighbour as yourself'.

But Jesus does more. You and I are religious people and along with other religious people such as Muslims, Sikhs, followers of Judaism and many others, we believe in the one God who created the Universe and all Humankind. But in addition, we are called 'Christians' because we believe that Jesus, the son born to a Palestinian woman named Mary in a town called Bethlehem over 1,990 years ago, is the full human expression of this God; we believe that when we want to know God, to hear Him to know God's mind, we need look no further than Jesus. Jesus is so much at one with God, that he has invited His followers to call God 'Father' – 'My Father and your Father'. He told His disciples: 'He that has seen *Me* has seen the Father'. God had promised His people that He would send them a 'Christ' for just this purpose. Because we believe Jesus to be that Christ, we believe in Him and are called 'Christians'.

To believe *in* Jesus is rather different from believing facts about Him. Many people believe the facts about Jesus – that He lived and died, that people looked up to Him, that He was a good man who helped others and so on, but such belief doesn't make them Christians – they believe the same about William Shakespeare and Sir Winston Churchill!

But to believe *in* Jesus is to believe:-

1) that human life has meaning and purpose; we are not in this world by accident;

2) that the world is built on moral foundations so there is right and there is wrong; our actions matter, and our moral standard is the mind of Christ;
3) that each one of us is important, but no more and no less so than the other people God has made; so we should not then think too highly of ourselves and too little of other people;
4) that we should order our lives on these beliefs, and let others know that we do so, in order that as they come to accept Jesus as Lord, greater and greater should be that alignment of human activity with God's will and purpose which we call the Kingdom of Heaven on earth.

In other words [in theological language], we believe Jesus to be the interpretation of all human life and history.

For His part, Jesus assures us of His commitment to us, by giving us his Holy Spirit to inspire, strengthen, and encourage us. His grace works in our hearts, and we respond by coming forward for baptism, in which we are marked forever as His own. Then, in Confirmation, through prayer and the laying-on of the Bishop's hands, His Holy Spirit confirms and strengthens His work in our hearts.

Today you have come to be strengthened – that is what Confirmation means. To confirm something is to strengthen it, to make it secure. In baptism Christ, through His Holy Spirit, marked you for His own, made you special, and today, through prayer and the laying-on of the Bishop's hands, the same Holy Spirit will strengthen what He has begun in you. It does not matter how you came to be here today – it may be that you felt that you make the world a better, kinder place; or it may be that you wanted something for yourself and you believed that the Church could provide it; or perhaps you came to keep someone else company. It does not matter – Christ speaks to different people in different ways when He calls them to Himself. What is more important is the knowledge that He is always more interested in what a man or woman with His help, can become, than in what he or she has been. He has called *you* and you are here to receive from him the grace necessary for whatever lies ahead. He will not leave you without the resources you will need to enjoy a fruitful Christian life. That is why He has provided the Holy Scriptures, especially the Gospels of Matthew, Mark, Luke and John. Prayerful reading of the Bible will help you to grow more and more in the likeness of Christ. Then there is the Holy Eucharist in which Christ is always present to feed us with his Body and Blood. And thirdly, there is the Fellowship of the Church with its liturgical recalling of Christ's saving acts and our future hope.

But even today as we rejoice that God has chosen you, and lavished his gifts upon you, we remember also that our God does not only call, he also sends. You first heard the good news of Jesus Christ through someone else – perhaps your parents or clergy or Sunday School teachers, neighbours or friends; now other people must hear about Him from you. You are not baptised and confirmed for yourself only. Christ is always calling people to Himself, to share the same joy you have in Him. But He calls them through those who are His friends. You are among His friends, and as we pray God's abundant blessings upon you, we pray also that by your own steadfast love for our Lord Jesus; your concern for all His sisters and brothers, particularly those who are so dear to His heart – the poor, the weak, the vulnerable and the sick; by the responsible way you deal with others in your life, private as well as public, in honesty, fairness, justice and love; by your constancy in private prayer and public worship, you will yourself be a blessing to many, many others – a true friend of Jesus in every way. This is our prayer for you today – your day of strengthening or Confirmation.

11

The Rev'd Guy Hewitt Presiding at the Eucharist for the First Time

Christ Church Parish Church, Barbados, 1 July 2005

Prayer: Spirit of the living God,
Fall afresh on us,
Break us, melt us, mould us, fill us and use us.

Amen

St John, chapter 21 verses 15-17
...Jesus saith to Simon Peter,
Simon, *son* of Jonas, lovest thou me more than these?
He saith unto him, Yea, Lord; thou knowest that I love thee.
He saith unto him, Feed my lambs.
He saith to him again the second time,
Simon, *son* of Jonas, lovest thou me?
He saith unto him, Yea, Lord; thou knowest that I love thee.
He saith unto him, Feed my sheep.
He saith unto him the third time,
Simon, *son* of Jonas, lovest thou me? Peter was grieved
because he said unto him the third time, Lovest thou me?
And he said unto him, Lord, thou knowest all things;
thou knowest that I love thee.
Jesus saith unto him, Feed my sheep.

The earthly ministry of our Lord Jesus Christ had but one purpose, namely to bring the whole world into the right relationship with God. This right relationship with God He called the Kingdom of Heaven and when He began His ministry people found this teaching so exciting that they followed Him in thousands to hear Him. When He sneaked off into the desert for a little quiet they tracked Him down and He had to teach them there. When He walked by the lakeside they crowded Him and He had to get into a boat and teach them from the boat. When He crossed the lake in a boat some followed Him in other boats while others hurried around by land to reach Him on the other side. They couldn't get enough of Him. At one stage He was able to send out seventy in pairs to take His teaching to places He had not been Himself. And then things changed. The crowds fell away. Perhaps some of them were bored with hearing the same teaching over and over again. The Kingdom of Heaven is like this, the Kingdom of Heaven is like that. Perhaps some of them were disappointed that He did not produce loaves and fishes every time they went to hear Him as He did on at least one occasion. And for some the final straw – the straw that broke the camel's back – was when He said 'unless you eat My flesh and drink My blood you have no life in you.' They said, 'This is a hard saying, who can take that?' and they went away.

And so it was that by the time of His death and Resurrection there were left only about 120 of them who had been with Him from the beginning and it was to this small company of the Faithful that He gave the task of continuing His work of bringing men and women into that right relationship with God which He called the Kingdom of Heaven on earth. The risen Christ identified Himself so completely with His Church on earth that when He confronted Saul on the Damascus road He did not say 'you are persecuting my friends', or 'you are persecuting my followers.' He said to Saul 'I am Jesus and you are persecuting Me.' Small wonder that theologians have called the Church the extension of the Incarnation.

Partly because of persecution and partly through missionary zeal the Church spread from Jerusalem and Palestine into every corner of the known world. As it spread, it grew in numbers as many converts joined and were called Christians. And wherever the Church was to be found, whether in large numbers or small, there were five discernible features, which are listed in the Acts of the Apostles, chapter 2 verse 42, viz: (1) the Church met constantly; (2) to hear the Apostles teach; (3) to share the common life; (4) to break bread, and (5) to pray. Christ gave to His Church for its work on earth three specific gifts. Firstly, life in His Spirit; secondly, His body and blood under the forms of bread and wine to feed this life; and thirdly a corps or cadre of servant shepherds to feed the Church with the food He provided. Theirs would be a thankless task so they had to be people who would give their all even to the point of their lives as He himself had done, and then would say we are unprofitable servants, we have only done our duty. In other words, it had to be a labour of love. Love for Christ himself.

So when Christ addressed and commissioned them by speaking to Peter, He said to Peter, 'Do you love Me? Then love Me by feeding My sheep'. We, you and I, are the Church and the Church exists to serve the Kingdom and the ministry is provided to serve the Church. Woe betide us if we get this the wrong way round and behave as though the Church should lord it over the world, and the clergy should lord it over the Church.

Today the Church gives to these servant shepherds the name of priests and their duties are described at the time of their ordination in the following or similar words:

Priests are called by God to work with the Bishop and their fellow priests as servants and shepherds among the people to whom they are sent. They are to proclaim the word of the Lord, to call their hearers to repentance and in Christ's name to absolve and declare the forgiveness of sins. They are to baptise and prepare the baptised for confirmation. They are to preside at the celebration of Holy Communion, to lead their people in prayer and worship, to intercede for them; to bless them in the name of the Lord, and to teach and encourage by word and example. They are to minister to the sick and prepare the dying for their death. They are to set the Good Shepherd always before them as the pattern of their calling, caring for the people committed to their charge and joining with them in a common witness to the world.

These duties may be grouped under four headings with the letters W-I-S and E.

W is for the Word of God. The priest must feed the flock on the Word of God in Holy Scripture. This means prayerful and careful reading and study of the Bible, so that they are able to refute error and express their faith with confidence. They must be able when someone says, the Bible says 'render your heart and not your garment' to explain that the Bible says rend meaning tear your heart and not your garment because there was the custom of wearing torn clothing with ashes on your head to show sorrow for wrong-doing, and Christ was saying that repentance should be of the heart and not in appearance only. They should be able to say when someone says, the Bible says 'money is the root of all evil' that what the Bible says is 'the love of money is the root of all evil', and when a misguided preacher thunders, 'and my friends when Jonah swallowed that whale,' they can point out, no my brother it was 'the whale that swallowed Jonah!' The priest must teach that the Bible is the inspired record of God's revelation of Himself to human beings in human situations, a revelation that is seen supremely in the life, death and Resurrection of our Lord Jesus Christ. But the Bible is not a magic book. It was a right instinct that caused people to place an open bible in a baby's cot before the baby was christened because it showed that the child, like the rest of us, is under God's loving protection, even before the child is baptized into the Christian family.

I is for Instruction in prayer and worship. The priest must teach the people that prayer is more than asking God for gifts. Rather prayer has to do with thinking the thoughts of Christ, of seeing the world and the people in it through His eyes, and so growing more and more into His likeness. Often there is no need for many words in prayer as though we are providing God with information, and giving Him instructions about what He should be doing, because the substance of prayer is not knowledge. The substance of prayer is love. There is the lovely story of the man who went often into church to sit for long periods with a smile on his face looking at Christ on the Cross, and when he was asked why he did this he replied, 'I look at Him, and He looks at me and we are happy together.' That, too, is a form of prayer.

The priest must also instruct the people in worship. The priest must teach the people that worship is more than religious entertainment. Religious entertainment has its place. Sacred concerts and cantatas provide the opportunity for individuals to give God thanks by displaying the talents He has given them in voice, musical ability, poetry, dance and drama. And because in doing so they also entertain us we rightly compliment them and applaud their efforts. But worship is not people-centred, but God-centred. In worship we reflect God's majesty and His mercy, His goodness, generosity and graciousness, and we see ourselves as recipients of His bounty, not through our merits, but because of His love. So whether we be queen, president, governor-general, prime minister, or Glendairy prison inmate, we are all God's children in God's house, and such distinctions are out of place. It is a deplorable trend to have politicians and others who are considered 'big-ups' display their wares and manifestos during church services when all should be sitting at the feet of Jesus in humility and gratitude.

S is for ministry to the Sick, and the Sacrament of Holy Communion. There are two reasons for Christians to do anything; first, because Christ did it and we are following His example; and second, because Christ says that we should do it and we are obeying His command. Both apply to ministry to the sick and to sharing in the Eucharist. Christ healed the sick and sent His followers to heal the sick; and on the night before He gave His life for us Christ gathered His friends around Him. He took bread and wine, gave thanks, and gave it to them saying, 'this is my body, this is my blood given for you, do this in remembrance of me'. So the Eucharist is the most perfect prayer there is. It has been celebrated in grand cathedrals, in the presence of kings and queens and in caves in the ground by a few frightened Christians expecting any moment to be arrested and thrown to the lions; it has been celebrated in the open air with thousands of people and hundreds of concelebrating priests, and it has been celebrated in a hovel, in a slum by the bedside of an old person dying in poverty; on battlefields by soldiers before going to certain death, and in prison camps, schools and colleges. Always the same Eucharist with the same infallible guarantee of Christ's presence. And for the priest the supreme, humbling and exhilarating experience of standing for a brief moment in the place of Christ and speaking the words of the Redeemer to those who have been redeemed. 'This is My body, this is my Blood, given for you, do this in remembrance of Me'.

E is for Encouragement by example. The priest must feed the flock in doing the right and avoiding the wrong, and by practising what he or she preaches. After all, it is still true that greater faith has no man than the bald headed man who buys hair restorer from a bald headed salesman. The priest must be an example of godly living. This will often mean self-denial as St Paul reminded the Christians in Corinth 'All things are lawful unto me but not all things are helpful.' There is one particular example the priest must set. Life in Barbados is plagued by gossip and rumour mongering, and sadly, Christian folk are as guilty as others in this respect. The priest must ensure that before he or she repeats a story that the threefold test is applied. First, is it true? Secondly, is it kind? If it is true and kind it may be repeated. If it is true but not kind, then the third question must be asked. Is it necessary? Because sometimes in order to avoid hurt and damage to other persons who must be warned, it is necessary to repeat a story that is true but not kind. The priest must always remember the African proverb, 'no flies can enter a closed mouth.'

To sum up then, Christ preached the Kingdom of Heaven and called His Church into being to continue this ministry. He gave the Church life in His Spirit, the Eucharist, and the Priesthood. Five indispensable features of the Church in any place should be constant meeting, apostolic teaching, sharing the common life, the Eucharist and prayer. Priests should be faithful to their calling by teaching the Word of God, instructing the Church in prayer and worship, ministering to the sick and celebrating the Holy Communion, and encouraging the Church by personal example of godly living. Such a priest is a wise priest. The Church is the servant of the Kingdom, not its ruler, and the clergy are the servants of the Church, not its masters.

But how is it that almost 2,000 years after Christ's sacrificial death and of the Church's existence the tares of injustice and sin seem to be choking the wheat of godliness and love? Could it be that the Church is failing in its mission and that this failure is due to the failure of the clergy? Certainly that is how some critics see it, and one such critic has remarked, 'It is no longer true that the hungry sheep look up and are not fed, rather the hungry sheep are fed up and no longer look.' Here in our own small corner of the world and the church, life in Barbados has many pleasant features, but it also has some blemishes which should not exist in a society where places of Christian worship are crowded Sunday by Sunday, and about which the Church should be concerned and should be registering this concern. For example, there is the all pervasive every-man-for-himself mentality; there is the fear of victimisation and consequently, silence in the face of injustice and inequality which leaves the weak defenceless against the strong and influential; there is the crudity and vulgarity masquerading as culture alongside the self-congratulatory talk of quality and excellence, and there are the low professional and business ethical standards, and lax personal morals. In such a climate the priest may have to choose between what the people want the priest to be, and what God wants the priest to be. The people may want the priest to be clever, rabble-rousing, entertaining, eloquent and popular. That spells CREEP, C-R-E-E-P, and a creep is someone who will say anything or do anything in order to curry favour, but the priest must not pride himself or herself on personal popularity and the high numbers he or she attracts because Christ told Peter to feed His sheep, He didn't tell him to count them, for God wants servant shepherds of His flock who are W-I-S-E.

At this season of Petertide, God makes to the Church in many countries a gift of new priests. Here in Barbados we have been given three new priests. They cannot undertake this great task in their own strength alone, they need Christ's strength and the prayers of His Church. So it is now up to us to show to Davidson, Sandra and Guy by our love and respect what high expectations we have of them, and to uphold them in prayer that God's purpose may be worked out in their lives, and being found faithful in their high calling they may play their part in advancing the Kingdom of Heaven on earth. Amen.

12
Tribute to David Udo on his Retirement

outgoing Director of
Southwark Diocese Race Relations Commission
Lambeth Methodist Church, London, UK, 5 May 1998

Joshua, chapter 24 verse 15
...choose you this day whom ye will serve; whether the gods which your fathers served that *were* on the other side of the flood, or the gods of the Amorites, in whose land ye dwell: but as for me and my house, we will serve the LORD.

There is, recorded in the twenty-fourth chapter of the Old Testament Book of Joshua, a remarkable and instructive incident. It occurred when the veteran Joshua, for so many years the respected leader of the Hebrew people, was on his deathbed. And these were the final words he spoke to the people he had loved and led for so long. He told them: *If you will not serve God, then choose today* whom *you will serve. Either the gods of your forefathers, or the gods of the Amorites in whose land you dwell. But as for me and my house – we will serve the* Lord.

Joshua *knew* his people. He knew that although in *theory* they acknowledged a God who would not be seen, and therefore had to be followed by faith only, in *practice* they only felt secure when there was in evidence some charismatic person they could call their 'leader'. For years he had filled this role but now he was dying, and there was no obvious successor. So Joshua knew that his people's temptation would be to say – 'no leader, no God'. He therefore outlined the alternatives before them. They could either try to bring back the old days – the days before they acknowledged that God was God; or they could discard their own distinctive beliefs, and accept the beliefs of the majority of people around them. He was not recommending either of these alternatives, so he was going to make it clear: the choice was theirs, but as for him and *his* house, he was going to serve the Lord. It was a *crucial* moment in the life of the Hebrew people.

Now, to be alive is to be vulnerable to change and to decision-making. So crucial moments are a normal part of life, and a crucial moment need not be a crisis. Crucial moments only become crises when men and women lose their faith in the ultimate triumph of good over evil; of peace over strife; of generosity over greed: when they abandon their search for the *end* because they do not immediately see the *means* to the end; and when they turn aside from the path which they know to be right, because they cannot see the next stepping stone. It is the lack of faith which transforms a crucial moment in a crisis.

But if we examine the alternatives that are set before us – that is the alternative faith – we see that these alternatives offer no greater security.

First, we are forced to recognise that people and events change and move on, and the past remains in the past. To try to squeeze ourselves back into the past, is simply not on.

Neither is the second alternative – that of trying to deny those personal convictions which we have, but the majority of our friends and workmates do not share, and to lose ourselves in the crowd around us – that is no way forward either. There *are* certain things that can be decided by a majority vote, but *truth* is not one of them. The earth was moving around the sun even in the days when only one man in the whole world believed this was so, and when everyone else believed that it was the sun that moved around the earth. So if today, we find that we are out of step with most of the people around us: for instance that we still believe in treating every other human being as our equal; that we still believe that life in Christ extends beyond the grave – we must still say: As for me and my house, we will serve the Lord. We must say this because we believe that in Jesus Christ, the Living Word of God, the very meaning of God whose life, death and Resurrection enable us to enter into the life and purpose of God, we have the assurance that *we can win through.*

To a particular group of Christians in the 1960s and since, the challenge to faith has taken particular form. These were Christians, who for the most part were nurtured in Christian homes in a Christian environment. Their role models in public life – statesmen, civil servants, teachers and religious leaders all acknowledged the place of God in human affairs, and because some such leaders were white, some were black and many were double-ethnic, it was easy to believe that all human beings were equal in God's love, and that Christians were people who were first and foremost brothers and sisters in Christ and whose skin colour made no difference to their witness. Understandably people nurtured in such an environment were devastated to arrive here from countries in the Caribbean and Africa and discover that here in England from which so many of these preachers had come, the ideal and practice of Christian brotherhood and sisterhood came a poor second to notions of white 'kith and kin'. In this country Church membership did not inhibit people from open support for the murderous racist regimes of Ian Smith in Rhodesia and apartheid in South Africa, or hailing as a stalwart Christian, the late Enoch Powell, who, even while physical attacks on black people, and intimidating demonstrations by racist mobs against the presence of black people in this country were going on, could be delivering the Holy Week addresses on the BBC while at the same time campaigning for the repatriation of black immigrants, many of whom were fellow Christians.

Sadly, this challenge to the Christian faith of some black Christians proved too great. Many of us know friends who were keen members of the Church in Africa and the Caribbean who after unsuccessful attempts to find a welcome in churches here rejected the Christian faith altogether. Many became agnostic, some atheist, some flirted with Marxism; a few took refuge in Rastafarianism, and a vocal minority shouted black power and revolution. Thankfully, by far the greatest number were able to distinguish between the living Lord Jesus who walked and talked with them, and Church members who merely said 'Lord, Lord'. They were led to form small house groups to read the Bible together, pray and generally encourage one another. These groups became the nucleus of today's Black Majority Churches, providing a Sunday haven from the six-day exposure to discrimination, rejection and downright hostility.

But there were also some outstanding and unrecognised stalwarts who refused to be enticed away, or driven off, the solid rock of Jesus Christ on whom they stood. They craved no publicity, and did not aspire to be 'leaders'. They had little or no quarrel with Socialism, Marxism, Rastafarianism, Sectarianism or the other 'isms' made so attractive by the racism of weak Christians, but they were convinced that racism and God's Holy Spirit are incompatible, and cannot co-exist, either in the human heart or in the Church, if either is true to the Lord Jesus. Racism is sin; to combat it is a divine calling, a vocation for the Christian, be he or she Methodist, Anglican, Roman Catholic or anything else, lay or ordained, paid worker or volunteer. It is a Christian witness to which they dedicated their lives. Like Martin Luther they said: 'Here I stand, I can do no other' and they echo the conviction of Martin Luther King.' 'We shall overcome some day.'

One such stalwart is David Udo, for whose ministry as Director of our Southwark Diocese Race Relations Commission we are giving thanks to God in this service, a truly unsung hero. It is not because he is ignorant of the methods of self-publicity or because he is afraid of confrontation that his ministry has largely remained a hidden one. Rather because he has modelled his ministry on that of a patient Jesus, who listened, probed with a gentle questioning, submitted to the arrogance of ignorance while doing his best to educate, and accepted suffering at the hands of those for whose liberation he was spending his life.

It is fortuitous that earlier this year David delivered the 11th Annual Martin Luther King Memorial lecture which has just been published and is now available for sale. In it he makes reference to some crucial events for the black community in this country in the sixties and seventies, but typically makes no mention of the part he himself played in these events. This must await the emergence of some perceptive chronicler whose attention is engaged by such events as the Olive Morris arrest and trial, the New Cross Massacre Campaign and the Stephen Lawrence murder.

His fifteen years as Director of Southwark Diocese Race Relations Commission are only a part, and may not even be the most productive part of his witness and ministry. There may well be other and more productive vehicles for the way God chooses to use him. While others seek to grab headlines, devise soundbites and compromise with structures of injustice, he will continue to see himself, not as a leader, but as a servant, who because he knows it is Jesus he is serving, will always count himself an unprofitable servant. Like Joshua, he will not presume to dictate to others. Like him he will say to them: '*You* can live in the past, *you* can worship the transitory goods of short-lived "success", but as for me and my house, we will serve the Lord.' We thank God for him and for the blessings of his continuing ministry.

13
Twenty-Five Years a Priest
Rev'd Stephen Dando

Thanksgiving Eucharist
St Lawrence Church, Eastcote, UK, 30 September 2009

It is a great privilege, and one for which I thank God, to be able to join you here in St Lawrence on this occasion, and I also thank the Rev'd Stephen Dando for inviting me to preach. Some of you may know that when I became Vicar of St Laurence, Catford in the Southwark diocese, one of my earliest and most pleasant tasks was to officiate at the wedding of Stephen and Elaine. They both became active workers for Christ in His Church in that parish, with Stephen serving as churchwarden, and Elaine as founder of the church's playgroup. Their vocations later converged in the Priesthood, and this evening we are celebrating the 25th anniversary of Stephen's ordination. Elaine will have to wait a few years longer for hers, but waiting has never deterred her!

Let us pray. Come Holy Spirit, and kindle in us such love for the Word of God that it may dwell in our hearts richly, and be a lantern to our feet and a light to our paths. AMEN.

First Epistle of St Peter, chapter 2 verse 9: *You are a chosen People, a Royal Priesthood, a dedicated Nation* ...

Some of us are careful, when petitioning the Almighty for His help for people we know to be in need, not to say 'especially So and So.' This is because we do not want to give the impression that there are limits to God's time and compassion and we want our own people and concerns to be at the front of the queue, or even that our concerns are of greater importance or urgency than others. Since in intercession we are trying to see the world through the eyes of Jesus, and aligning our will with His, the word we use is 'particularly' because the persons and causes known to us are but particulars of many such not known to us, but who are all equal in God's love. Particularity, not exclusivity has always been the hallmark of God's dealings with us.

The priesthood of any individual priest is but the particularity of the Priesthood of the whole people of God, conferred on it by Christ Himself. In sundry religions, priesthood is the offering of sacrifice to a god or gods. Someone is designated to officiate at the ritual, and he is called the priest. Whatever is offered, be it animal or object or even human, is called the victim. The Priesthood of Christ differs from all other versions of priesthood in that the Incarnate Son of God is Himself both Priest and Victim, and it is this priesthood that He has conferred upon the whole People of God. So even as we give thanks to God for calling His servant Stephen to the office of Priest in His Church, we give Him even greater thanks for the Church itself. Stephen is a faithful priest insofar as he exhibits in his personal life and ministry the characteristics of the essential nature of the Church.

Three Anglican divines of the twentieth century provide us with descriptions of the nature and calling of the Church. The first is Bishop John Robinson of 'Honest to God' fame. He stated: 'We can have as high a doctrine of the ministry as we like, provided our doctrine of the Church is higher; and we can have as high a doctrine of the Church as we like, provided our doctrine of the Kingdom is higher.'

The second is Archbishop William Temple. He stated: 'The Church of God is the only institution that exists for those who are not its members.'

The third is Archbishop Michael Ramsey. He stated: 'The Church lives towards God, and towards the world. Towards God it worships. Towards the world, it preaches the Gospel; it reconciles persons with God and therefore with one another; it infects the world with righteousness; it embodies the divine principles on which human life is ordered.'

First, Worship. From the earliest times the Church could not hide itself among nondescript groups because of the uniqueness of its worship. It worshipped the one true God and could not compromise by accepting the Roman Emperor or any one else as a deity, but held that the one true God had taken human flesh in the person of Jesus Christ who was to be worshipped as God. It was its worship that made the Church subject to persecution, a pariah among religious groups, and very lonely. Yet the Church could neither abandon nor compromise on this very reason for existence. It should be the same today. The first duty of the priest does not lie in efficient management or even in community activism, important as these may be, but in the dedication of his or her life, and the lives of those committed to his or her care to the worship of God in Christ, whatever the cost in isolation or ridicule.

It is the greatest paradox that the biggest bane of the priestly life is loneliness, and its antidote is to be alone! Jesus found that the antidote for the clamour of the crowds for food and healing, for the hostility of the religious and secular powers, and even for the rigours of teaching about the Kingdom of God which seemed incomprehensible even to His closest followers, was time spent alone with the Father. So exclusive time with God, for the priest in prayer, and for the People of God in worship, is paramount. Whatever may be the passing fashions of the secular world, the Church at worship must exhibit a reverence, a sense of awe which betokens the presence of One who is Almighty yet accessible, majestic yet merciful, just yet compassionate. The loving care with which the priest handles Word and Sacrament as he or she leads a grateful, forgiven people in praise and thanksgiving will be indicative of worship which we hope is acceptable to our loving Father.

Secondly, the Church preaches the Gospel. What is this gospel or good news? The sacrificial love of God. The good news that God loved and loves the world He has made, that He gave and gives Himself in the sacrificial love of His Son Jesus Christ, that whoever has faith in Him or genuinely desires to have faith in Him will receive His Holy Spirit and the eternal life which this brings. Church and Priest preach this good news, which cannot be conveyed by speech alone, but by the offering of their own lives.

Thirdly, the Church reconciles persons to God and therefore to one another. Most of us are familiar with Our Lord's parable of the Prodigal Son, the wastrel boy who received a warm and forgiving welcome from his father when he recognised and regretted his wrongdoing and turned towards his father. In a church office in New York I came across a notice which read: 'This church welcomes you regardless of your colour, class, gender or the number of times you have been born!' The Church fears neither sin nor the sinner because Christ is the answer to both. An encounter with Christ may take place anywhere and any time – at work, leisure, home, or in any activity. Such an encounter reveals the light of Christ's self-giving love, and in that light we see ourselves as invited into His embrace. When we are humble enough to accept that embrace however unworthy we know ourselves to be, we are drawn into a fellowship with those who also know themselves to be ransomed, healed, restored and forgiven. The Church is that welcoming fellowship, not necessarily a group of like-minded persons, but who know themselves to be loved by God, and who want very much to love others.

Fourthly, the Church must infect the world with righteousness. The Lord Jesus has said that we are the salt whose saltiness must savour the world. Having bestowed upon the Church the gift of His Holy Spirit, God expects the Church to bring forth the fruit of the Spirit. So love, joy, peace, patience, goodness, kindness, faithfulness, gentleness and self-control must exude from the Church into the wider society. In this way there should emerge a public structure of truth in which morality wipes out greed and graft, corruption and exploitation, and replaces dishonest acquisition of riches, fame and success with integrity and respect for others.

Fifthly, the Church embodies divine principles on which human life is ordered. St Paul identifies these principles as Faith, Hope and Love. Faith is the conviction that despite all signs to the contrary, the world is built on moral foundations, and that in the end it will be well with the good and ill with the wicked. Hope is the assurance given by the Resurrection of Jesus that we too, may pass through death to fall into the arms of a loving God. Love is that communion of extreme mutual self-giving.

Such then is the glory of the Church in its call to worship and witness. This glory shines in every act of love and kindness by every member of Christ's body living out his or her baptismal promise to be faithful to Him who has called us out of darkness into His marvellous light.

We bring the offering of our whole lives when we accept the invitation of Christ to assemble, take bread and wine, give thanks, break and share. He Himself invites: 'Eat this bread and drink this wine. It is my body and my blood, given for the forgiveness of your sins.' And to be chosen to speak Our Lord's words in His Name on such occasions is the highest of privileges.

This evening we rejoice with Stephen in thanksgiving for twenty-five years of exercising and enjoying this privilege. This occasion demands of those among us who have been similarly privileged, to join Stephen in bowing low before Our crucified Lord in humble adoration and gratitude, and praying that we may be daily renewed in faith all the remaining days of our lives to serve Him as He asks of us, whatever the cost may be. It is that to which we have been called. Its other name is 'holiness.'

14
Jo and Denis Stanley

Homily read at the funeral service of
Josephine Mary Stanley
Kingsdown Crematorium, Swindon, UK
2 September 2008

A short phrase of two words only, describes completely Christian faith and Christian life. That phrase is 'Sacrificial Love.' Each word defines the other, and together they describe Christian belief and practice. They also describe how Denis and Jo related to each other, and how together they related to Christine, Tony and Jeremy. I do not believe that they would have described what they had together in those words, or even that they would have stopped to describe it at all, but that is what it was, a gift they received from God because they were open to receive it.

Many people find it easy to believe that the God Who created them loves them. What they find difficult to believe is that the same God loves everyone else no more and no less. So they have difficulty in accepting people as they are. It was one of Jo's greatest attributes that she was able to accept people, and enjoy people without ever feeling the need to refashion them in her or anyone else's image. She respected other people's space, not because she was undiscerning or uncaring, but because she recognised that they were entitled to their own place in God's creation as she was entitled to hers. She lived by that scriptural code which is sometimes called 'The Golden Rule', namely, 'Do unto others as you would have them do unto you.' It requires strength of character to do this, and Jo was a very strong character.

Over the years that strength of character has upheld many people, myself included. From our first meeting in 1973 up to her heavenly birthday on the 23rd of this month her friendship along with Denis's with my wife and me, and with our children as they grew to maturity, and her support for my ministry has been unshakeable, effective and deeply appreciated.

In 1974 St Laurence, Catford was to be my first cure and I was to be its first black vicar. The early 1970s were a period of some unrest as the country tried to come to terms with its new black permanent presence. Twelve years of ordained ministry had taught me that even in the Church things are not always what they seem. A veneer of politeness can mask resentment or even hostility. Jo and Denis were a tower of strength, not only in what they did but in what they were. Completely free of any racial prejudice, there was no pretence about them. They had a respect for truth and the security of being honest which enabled them to offer constructive criticism and to point out mis-judgements without being patronising. I shall always be grateful. It is a measure of how much Jo loved us that while dreading a long plane journey she made the sacrifice in order to visit us in Barbados last November.

Sunday after Sunday in St Laurence Church Jo prayed to the God to Whom all hearts are open and from Whom no secrets are hidden. She received at Christ's hands the spiritual food of His Body and Blood as pledges of the life to come. We know that she has fallen into the arms of a loving God, and we believe that she has passed from life to life. We do not know what St Peter will make of that husky greeting: 'Hello darling' but she will be most welcome. May she rest in Christ and be raised with Him in glory.

May Denis, Christine, Tony and Jeremy, Minty, Molly and Jean, and their respective families and all who knew and love Jo find comfort in the abiding presence of Christ with them, and encouragement in the knowledge that death is no barrier to love.

15
Requiem Mass for the Rt Rev'd Lord David Sheppard

formerly Suffragan Bishop of Woolwich, Southwark and
Diocesan Bishop of Liverpool
Southwark Cathedral, UK, 22 March 2005

St Matthew, chapter 6 verse 33
But seek ye first the kingdom of God,
and his righteousness; and all these things
shall be added unto you.

David Sheppard's life was a missionary life. Christian mission has been defined as 'ministry within a dimension of difference'. David Sheppard was not born and bred on Merseyside; he was not a Roman Catholic; he was not a victim of urban poverty; he was never unemployed; he was not 'gay' and he was not black. But in these our several communities we who knew him at first hand, can testify that in our quest for fair play in British society and God's world he walked with us, alongside us and among us in partnership without patronising, with a sympathy that was neither synthetic nor sentimental and with a commitment that was born of conviction. And whoever were his companions, his was always a journey for God's kingdom of justice.

I vividly recall the occasion when I first heard the name of David Sheppard. Fifty-five years ago I was a thirteen-year old schoolboy in Barbados watching an after-school football match in Queens Park when the news came through that our 1950 West Indies cricket team which was then touring England had been put to the sword by Cambridge University. The University's opening pair had put on 343 runs before a wicket fell. Johnny Dewes got a century; but the real destroyer of the West Indies bowling with a personal score of 227 was a young man named David Sheppard. Little did I know then that the Lord Jesus would call that young man to serve others in His name as an ordained minister of the Church of England, or that I too would receive a similar call. Some years after that the killing of the West Indian Kelso Cochrane and the Notting Hill Race Riots so-called prompted me to travel to England to serve in a parish in Shepherd's Bush, one mile west of Notting Hill, and when David Sheppard became Bishop of Woolwich, with the characteristic humility that was in the marrow of his bones, he asked if he could come and spend some time with me while I went about my work. Thus began a friendship which saw us campaign together against apartheid in South Africa, saw me work with him and succeed him as Chairman of the Martin Luther King Memorial Trust, saw him institute me as Vicar of St Laurence, Catford, in this diocese of Southwark, saw my family and me spend many happy summer holidays in Bishop's Lodge through the courtesy of David and his wife Grace, and eventually saw me join him in the Episcopal ranks of the Church of England.

There is a sense in which, as the world views success, David Sheppard achieved a notable Triple First. In sport to become captain of England at cricket; in public life become a Peer of the realm, and in ecclesiastical preferment an outstanding diocesan bishop, only narrowly missing out on the Archbishopric of Canterbury. It would be easy for the less perceptive to think that this was always in the stars for a gifted and personable young man who was born into a solid middle class family, and had a public school education as a springboard to such goals which were achieved with effortless ease. But that would be a superficial reading of a life in which although honour, duty, service and sacrifice were writ deep, these were not the result of cold showers and severe beatings, but the outcrop of a deep love for the Lord Jesus whose Incarnation elevated humanity and made us too precious in God's sight to be dehumanised by poverty, bigotry, greed and exploitation.

It would also be to misunderstand the nature of the call to which David had responded. In early religions the priests offered, on behalf of the people and themselves, sacrifices of living or inanimate victims. But the priesthood of Christ was different in that with Christ priest and victim were one and the same. And Christian priesthood is of that priesthood of Christ. So suffering is an inescapable element of faithful Christian priesthood. And David was a faithful Christian priest.

Those closest to David and Grace had some inkling of the cost of their discipleship for David had his detractors, but they were not ones to complain and only the occasional comment said with a wry smile 'It has been warm in the kitchen recently' – a reference to the slogan 'if you can't stand the heat get out of the kitchen' would indicate how tough things were from time to time. But they were mature enough to understand that in today's social and political climate when the freewheeling individual can achieve great wealth and prominence through arms trafficking, insider trading and pornography, and when war making world leaders jettison Christian moral standards to countenance as 'collateral damage' the calculated killing of civilians, including women and children, and when in the comfort of our armchairs we find entertainment and gratification in the public humiliation and degradation of people for money on television game shows, such a high profile stand for the dignity and worth of human personality would attract scoffers and even a measure of hostility. But it may be that future generations will recall the name of David Sheppard with the same sense of gratitude that we now recall the names of William Wilberforce, Elizabeth Fry, Lord Shaftesbury and Samuel Plimsoll, and be inspired in their day to make their own stand for the poor and wretched of the earth.

David Sheppard's personal encounter with the Lord Jesus at a missionary meeting, and his evangelical grounding in prayer and in Holy Scripture as the Word of God, left him in no doubt that he should spend his life sharing with others the good news of Jesus the Compassionate Christ. News that a loving God made man in His own image, that in Christ God reconciles men and women to Himself and therefore to one another, that humanity is redeemed from sin and its consequences by sacrificial love, and that the Resurrection of Jesus assures us that death is not the end, and that love will have the last word. It was only a matter of where and how he would be spreading this Gospel.

There is the apocryphal story of the traveller in the Sahara Desert who suddenly came across a hive of activity. There was machinery everywhere and men scurrying back and forth. He found the man who appeared to be in charge and asked what this activity was about. He replied 'I am building a rocket to shoot me to the top of the Himalayas.' 'And why do you want to go to the top of the Himalayas?' the traveller asked. 'Well, it is like this,' the man replied, 'I have a questing mind, you see, I have a questing mind. I like to solve problems. And I look around me here and I see all these problems, and I can't solve any of them, so I am going to find new ones.' Fortunately for us, David Sheppard did not choose to go to the far-flung corners of the earth to preach the Gospel. He did it here and now among us. We give thanks to God that he did.

My Training Vicar in Shepherd's Bush, the Rev'd Roderick Gibbs, once rolled up his trouser leg to show me with pride where a cover drive from David Sheppard had left a mark on his shin. David Sheppard's life and ministry have left even more significant marks on the life of our Church and Nation.

The Psalmist says that we human beings are fearfully and wonderfully made. Those of us who knew David Sheppard find this easy to believe. By all accounts he had the final blessing and grace of a holy death. May he rest in Christ and be raised with Him in glory. Amen.

16
Mrs Beatrice Ernesta Adams Née Norville

Sermon preached at her funeral
St Laurence Church, Catford, UK, 2 September 1997

1 Corinthians, chapter 15 verse 19
If in this life only we have hope in Christ, we are of all
men most miserable.

What is a Christian? Not merely someone who believes that there is a god – the devils also believe that. Not merely someone who believes *in* God. Many religious people, including Muslims, Sikhs, followers of Judaism and others believe *in* God. The Christian is one who believes in God; believes in a call to live in the Spirit of this Jesus; and relies for the necessary strength to do so, not on human device, wisdom or ability, but on God's grace.

To live in the Spirit of Jesus is to be in love with a God whose presence cannot be ascertained by sight, touch, smell, taste or hearing and whose reality can only be apprehended by faith. So the challenge to the Christian is to be rooted in a world circumscribed by sights, touch, smell, taste and hearing while at the same time living faithfully in a reality not so circumscribed. It is a challenge from Jesus to men and women to step into this reality which is His, and such life in His Kingdom, this life of grace, this supernatural life, when viewed from our human perspective is described as 'loving your neighbour as yourself.'

It may be that so to live in the Kingdom may have much in common with Gray's 'gem of purest ray serene which the dark unfathomed caves of ocean bear' or that 'flower born to blush unseen.' There may be no commanding presence, no brilliant intellect, no outstanding physical prowess, no Midas touch in the accumulation of wealth and power, no artistic genius – in short, none of the things which the world counts as greatness. So often where these are present, and those gifted with them then choose to be servants, such a choice adds to their own greatness and they receive further credit for their humility. But the truly humble person, living the life of the kingdom but shorn of the romance of self-emptying and the voluntary choice of poverty, must draw heavily upon the grace of God to remain steadfast in service of others to be forgiving in the face of the amused contempt, pity, ingratitude, betrayal, irritation, anger and even open hostility which other peoples' goodness arouses in some of us.

There are many joys which come with the exercise of ordained ministry in the Church, and one of them is that it brings into one's life, a higher than average number of such people. One is privileged to catch glimpses behind the scenes as it were, and to recognise the personal cost and suffering out of which such service comes. If one is perceptive, one recognises it for what it is – *sacrificial love* – which took the form of a cross once, but continues to take other forms in the lives of those who are his hands and feet among us.

I have known a number of such people, some of whom sat in these same pews, made communion at this altar rail and who now rejoice with Christ in a greater light and on a farther shore where no torment can touch them. Amy Borrett, Hilda Marsh, Ivy Marchant come to mind. Beatrice was one such person. If at a time like this we recall the immense sadnesses of her life it must only be in order to wonder at the resilience and quiet strength with which she overcame them. I can still remember her calm tone and her exact words when she telephoned me late on that night of October 12th almost eighteen years ago: 'This is Beatrice. I am at Lewisham Hospital. David is no longer with us.' Next morning we went together to the fateful spot in Canadian Avenue where he had come off the bike she had tried her best to dissuade him from acquiring. It had been raining and she looked down on her son's blood mingled with water. I have never heard her speak of it, but how often must that have come to her mind when she read or heard tell of the blood and water which poured from Our Lord's side when a soldier pierced him to make sure that he was dead. Or when as an altar server she watched the priest mingle water with the blood-red wine for the life-sustaining sacrament.

Beatrice sought no reward for her devotion to Christ, or for her service to His children – not even the reward of resurrection and life after death. It was enough for her to serve Christ as He desired,

> To give and not to count the cost,
> To fight and not to heed the wounds
> To toil and not to seek for rest,
> To labour and not ask for any reward
> Save that of knowing that she did His will.

Finally, Beatrice was one of twelve people who in 1985 pledged themselves to support my ministry in the Church by constant prayer. I doubt not that she remained faithful to that pledge, and that now, even nearer to the heart of Jesus, she continues to do so, for we know, that it is not for this life only that God has given us hope. We do not have words enough to thank God for Beatrice and we are confident that she rests in Christ to rise with him in glory.

17
Herbert Ross James
Homily read at his funeral service
Breakspear Crematorium, Ruislip, UK, 2 January 1997

Revelations, chapter 21 verse 7
He that overcometh shall inherit all things;
and I will be his God, and he shall be my son.

In one sense it is a pity, and in another sense, it is quite right that we have only twenty minutes for this service. It is a pity because twenty minutes is not time enough to do justice to a recitation of Bert's virtues, and the contribution he made in so many ways to so many lives. On the other hand it reminds us that he lived a Christian life as best he could, and although that is all that God requires of us all – to do the best we can – the rewards for that are not on this side of the grave. You remember the parable of the talents where Our Lord Jesus approved of the man who was given two talents and made two more, and the man who was given five and made five more. It is not the same total that is required from each, but a full effort with what he or she has been given. It is because Bert did just that, that we know his reward was not in this life – neither in material wealth, nor in honours or flattery, but is with Christ who knows the hearts of all men; who judges with mercy, and will reward wisely.

Today, I want to be the voice of the many hundreds of people whose lives were made a little easier because of Bert's tireless efforts to find ways of helping people in need. Some of you will know that he was the founder and driving force behind 'Infeld', the community organisation in West London which helps so many sick and elderly people to cope with bureaucracy in their struggle to keep a roof over their heads, keep themselves warm and to have something to eat without having to lose their dignity or sense of being somebody. And there are many people overseas who will never have heard the name 'Bert James' but whose life's chances were improved through Christian Aid contributions which year after year Bert organised. Many of you will know of his church work based at St Stephen with St Thomas, Shepherd's Bush, and some of you will know that almost single-handedly he constructed the little St Thomas Chapel under the bell-tower which enabled us clergy to avoid freezing to death in the open church when we said morning and evening prayers in the winter. There are many, many good neighbourly acts, far too numerous to mention that Bert performed without thought of reward or thanks. But I trust you will bear with me if I become personal in paying tribute to a really great man.

It was my good fortune when I was a green curate responsible for the parish branch of the AYPA (Anglican Young People's Association) to have Bert as one of my two adult helpers. I was newly arrived from the West Indies and he and Doris took me under their wing. Their home at 60 Loftus Road became a second home, and I well remember some of the many places we travelled together – Bert riding his motor-cycle, I clinging on behind sitting on the pillion, and believe it or not, Doris, Pauline, Philip and baby Alison, all in the side-car! Frensham Ponds, the Hog's Back on the A3, Virginia Water, Windsor Great Park, Hampton Court are only a few such places. It was the James family more than anyone else who helped me appreciate the basic decency, sense of fair play and neighbourly concern which are characteristic of the British working family at its very best. They could not know that they were helping to tutor a future bishop in the Church of God. While Enoch Powell fulminated, and dockers marched against immigration, the James family was steady as a rock, treating all people as God's children, created in His image. They never missed Sunday worship unless they couldn't help it, and during the week they never missed an opportunity to help another human being.

Bert of course was not alone. In some respects life gave him a rough deal, not least when his working life as a factory manager was cut short by serious and incapacitating injury sustained at work, and which necessitated many painful operations and many periods in hospital. But there is one sense in which Bert drew first prize – when God gave him Doris as his life's partner. Doris was a partner in every sense of the word. She pulled her weight; she carried him when he needed to be carried; she gave him reason to carry on when he was let down by others; she never allowed him to be sorry for himself when life dealt him some bitter blows. They were worthy parents of the happy, lovely children, Pauline, Philip and Alison, and their grandchildren can be proud of them.

None of us can ever repay Bert for all that he was and all that he did, and on the human level we grieve that this is so. All we can do is offer our condolences to all his family including his brothers and sisters, nephews and nieces, and we commend him to the loving care of our Heavenly Father. May he rest in Christ and rise with Him in glory. Amen.

18
The Rt Rev'd
Dr Herman Spence

Late Bishop of Kingston, Jamaica
Preached at his funeral at the Parish Church of
St Andrew, Half Way Tree, Kingston, Jamaica
11 October 2001

1 Samuel, chapter 3 verse 18
It is the LORD: let him do what seemeth him good.

There are times when much to the annoyance of the spectators who are enjoying a master batsman in full flow, the captain declares the innings closed and calls in his batsmen. The person least perturbed about this is the master batsman himself, who is not at the wicket for his own glory. He is as willing to stay at the crease as he is to leave. For him, it is the captain's decision that really matters. He has faith in his captain who was the person who picked him in the first place, and he knows that there is an even more important tour coming up – in another country. So while others grumble or rage, he says: he is the captain; the captain is in charge.

The peace of God passes all understanding. And not only His peace, but often many of His ways. We know this is His world, and that He must grieve at the way it is disfigured by human greed, cruelty and selfishness – our lack of love for Him and for our neighbour. Every night half of the people in the world go to bed hungry while elsewhere unwanted foodstuff is stored and destroyed; Every minute of every day, twenty people, eighteen of them children, die of starvation or malnutrition related diseases – the equivalent of a jumbo jet crashing every fifteen minutes and killing everyone on board. Yet every year the nations of the world spend billions of dollars on guns, bombs and making war. Such a world does not reflect God's love for his creation and badly needs the voices of God's prophets who will speak equally fearlessly to prince, politician, peasant, or pauper, saying 'God has shown us another and a better way'. Surely such a world needs more Herman Spences – not fewer!

But it is the Lord; let Him do what is good in His own eyes. For Herman Spence, sometime priest, pastor and bishop was essentially a *prophet*. Like that best known of all the prophets – John the Baptist – Herman knew that every one of us stands under God's judgement in the way we treat one another, and his passion for justice meant that he had no thought for his own life or safety when he identified wrongdoing and called for repentance.

Secondly, if like John the Baptist, he was at times fierce, he was also, like John the Baptist, a man of prayer. It is not always remembered that when the disciples of Jesus went to Him and asked Him to teach them to pray, the example the cited was John the Baptist. Lord, teach us to pray as John taught his disciples to pray. Herman had an insatiable longing for the kind of intimacy with Jesus which is only possible in prayer. So for him, the Eucharist was not merely a 'church service', but because of Christ's saving work, it is the overlap of time and eternity, in which, though still earthbound, he could know the reality and nearness of another dimension in which he is enfolded in the mystery of God. It is prayer of the highest order.

Thirdly, the plain speaking, prayerful John the Baptist, was really a humble man who never gave himself airs or got above his station. Although crowds flocked to him and he had many followers, he was careful not to allow himself to be the object or focus of their devotion. He pointed them all to Jesus. 'I am only a voice', he said – 'look, *there* is the Lamb of God'. John the Baptist had a strong sense of call – to be a servant pointing others to the Master.

Herman was a winsome personality, and it is not surprising that he inspired a strength of affection and loyalty on the part of some, who, consciously or unconsciously, caught through him a glimpse of the Person to whom he was pointing. But he too had a strong sense of call. He knew that it was by the grace of God that he was what he was. He had no wish to cultivate such affection or to exploit it for his own ends. It is significant and not surprising, that he asked that there should be no eulogy at this service. That is why there will be no long list of his virtues; no recitation of his academic and other achievements; no recalling of the many honours heaped upon him or the service he rendered to many. But there are many who would gladly bear witness, in spoken or written word, to the beneficial effect on their own lives; of his ministry, friendship and love. However, we trust that the many unsolicited testimonies that have been forthcoming, will in years to come afford to June, Christopher, Simone, Nicole and the other members of his family, some comfort in the knowledge that others are able to corroborate what they themselves knew at first hand.

But in this connection, I must share with you one of the greatest compliments I have ever been paid. Two days ago, in Croydon, England, I was speaking to some people about Herman and about the challenges he had faced in his ministry. I had concluded by saying 'He was loved by many, resented by few, and respected by all', when my secretary burst out; 'Hey! You are describing yourself!' If that is true, could it be that unconsciously I had modelled myself on Herman? – or more likely that together, we have been trying to live in imitation of that Lamb of God in whose direction John the Baptist pointed us as so many others?

Like John the Baptist, Herman Spence denounced wrongdoing, taught people to pray and pointed others to Jesus. Christ's Holy, Catholic and Apostolic Church was the abiding love of Herman's life. He saw the Church as God's appointed means of reconciling his whole creation to himself and so had generously given unworthy folk like himself a share in the work of this reconciliation. It was in that understanding, that he bore the hardships that came his way, because he knew from the example of Christ, that often the reconciler has to bear in his own body, the pain of those who are being reconciled. He saw the Church in Jamaica as the local expression of this universal Church with the same vocation, and had no hesitation in calling for the Church to take a proactive role in the political as well as the social life of this country. He know that part of the government's duty is to make it as easy as possible for men and women to live as God intends, and this included the dignity and self-respect of those considered poor in the world's eyes.

He held a very high doctrine of the Priesthood, but he also shared the view of the late Bishop John Robinson who said: 'You can have as high a doctrine of the ministry as you like – provided your doctrine of the Church is higher. And you can have as high a doctrine of the Church as you like – provided your doctrine of the Kingdom is higher.'

In all this he sought no reward – not even the reward of resurrection. For him it was doing the will of God that is important – doing it not for any kind of reward – material or spiritual, but because it *is* the will of God.

St Paul could have had Herman in mind when he wrote in 2 Corinthians, chapter 6 verses 3–10: *We put no stumbling block in anyone's path, so that our ministry will not be discredited. Rather, as servants of God, we commend ourselves in every way; in great endurance; in troubles, hardships and distresses; in beatings, imprisonment and riots; in hard work, sleepless nights and hunger; in purity, understanding, patience and kindness; in the Holy Spirit and sincere love; in truthful speech and in the power of God; with weapons of righteousness in the right hand and in the left; through glory and dishonour; bad report and good report; genuine yet regarded as imposters; known yet regarded as unknown; dying and yet we live on; beaten and yet not killed; sorrowful yet always rejoicing; poor yet making many rich; having nothing yet possessing all things.*

So I am confident that however much Herman has enjoyed his innings, when he knew that his captain was declaring his innings closed, his thoughts could be summed up in the words of our text: 'He is the Lord. Let Him do what is good in His own eyes.'

We must take our cue from him, and content ourselves with giving God thanks for enriching our lives, and the lives of many others, through his servant Herman. We had no inalienable *right* to have known or be loved by someone in whom the grace of God flowered in such profusion, but God Himself gave us this *privilege*. Give God the praise.

And so we take leave of him with the words of hope which the priest in the Confessional pronounces after he has absolved the penitent sinner: 'May the Passion of Our Lord Jesus Christ, the prayers and merits of Blessed Mary and all the Saints; whatsoever good you have done or evil you have endured, be acceptable to God in the forgiveness of your sin and His gift of eternal life.'

May he rest in Christ, and rise with Him in glory.

19
Hadley 'Lynn' Daniel

Preached at his funeral
Acton Baptist Church, London, UK, 31 August 1994

St John, chapter 1 verse 47
Jesus saw Nathanael coming to him, and saith of him,
Behold an Israelite indeed, in whom is no guile!

Nathaniel, who was also known as Bartholomew, was one of our Lord's twelve disciples who did not attract the attention of the crowds. Nowhere in the Gospels do you find him doing anything spectacular or asking for special favours or making promises he couldn't keep such as James and John and Peter. Yet Jesus who knew the hearts of all men, said of him: 'He is the real thing – there is nothing false about him.'

Every year the Church celebrates the life and witness of St Bartholomew on August 24, St Bartholomew's day, so when on the day after, we returned from Barbados to receive the sad and unexpected news that our dear friend Lynn had died, I felt that Our Lord's opinion of Bartholomew was also how we felt about Lynn – he was real and genuine – there was nothing false in him.

Like Bartholomew, Lynn was always content to make his contribution as part of the team, rather than seek personal recognition or glory or even thanks. But quite often the whole success of the team's work depended almost entirely on him, because it was *voluntary* work and sometimes other people felt free to give priority to other engagements, whereas he was entirely dependable. He was nearly always the most reliable, the most self-effacing and the most supportive member of any group he was working with. Above all, he was most *loyal,* and if Lynn ever had an adverse or derogatory opinion of anyone he must have kept it to himself, because I for one, in all the years I have known him, never heard him express such an opinion.

I know this from personal experience. Lynn was one of the twelve of us who formed the entire membership and first committee of the Shepherd's Bush Social and Welfare Association in 1967. In fact he was one of those who chose that name for the self-help enterprise we were launching. Over the following years eleven of us have dispersed – some returning to Barbados, Grenada and Guyana, others moving to the USA and other parts of this country. Out of it grew the Shepherd's Bush Credit Union, the Evening Classes and Supplementary School; the Day Nursery. It provided a home for the Kickstars Steel Band, and the once dilapidated St Thomas Hall is now a well-furnished facility where members of our community can meet, relax and entertain ourselves and others in security and comfort. And the one person who has been there from the beginning, through thick and thin, ups and downs, holding things together, while others came and went, and serving in virtually every office in the Association, from the first day until his untimely death just over a week ago, was Lynn – a model of stability and quiet strength – just the role model our young people so badly need today.

Present and future generations whose life chances are enhanced from benefits from the Association, from the Credit Union, from the Nursery and Supplementary School will never know how much they owe to the quiet man with the winsome smile who was always there to do the job other people shunned or fell down on. He was truly a man for others, who described himself as being 'only poor and civil'. In physical stature, he was small but a giant in every other way. For those with eyes to see, the source of his quiet strength was his deep Christian faith, his thankfulness for all that God had done for him and his love for the Lord Jesus, but he was the last person to wear his religion on his sleeve.

We thank God that before his death he was able to see his daughter Mandy, the apple of his eye, find happiness in marriage, and we can find it in our hearts to regret that should Peter and Mandy be blessed with children, they will not have known their lovely grandfather. But – the Lord gives and the Lord takes away; blessed be the name of the Lord.

We thank God that He enriched our lives with Lynn's companionship, love, wise counsel, service and example. St Paul may not have been thinking of Lynn Daniel, or that other great stalwart who passed away just eleven days before he did – Jestine Crawford – but he certainly described them in 2 Corinthians, chapter 6 when he said:

We recommend ourselves by the innocence of our behaviour, our grasp of truth, our patience and kindliness; by gifts of the Holy Spirit, by sincere love, by declaring the truth, by the power of God. We wield the weapons of righteousness in right hand and left. Honour and dishonour, praise and blame, are alike our lot: we are impostors who speak the truth, the unknown men whom all men know; dying we still live on; disciplined by suffering, we are not done to death; in our sorrows we have always cause for joy; poor ourselves, we bring wealth to many penniless, we own the world.

St Bartholomew's quiet manner did not prevent Christ from recognising his true worth. Neither did Lynn's. He was truly our St Bartholomew of West London. May He rest in Christ, and rise with Him in glory.

20
Farewell Address
to Croydon Archdeaconry

Croydon Parish Church, UK, 27 July 2002

St Mark, chapter 3 verse 14
And he ordained twelve, that they should be with him,
and that he might send them forth to preach,

When the eleven Apostles came to choose a replacement for Judas, the 'person profile' they used was that the person had to be someone who had walked with Jesus, and the 'job description' they used was that he was to be a witness to the Resurrection. These requirements followed almost exactly Jesus' own intentions when He chose the original Twelve, because we are told that 'He chose Twelve, in order (1) that they might be with Him and (2) that He might send them out.'

The Apostles made a shortlist of two, Matthias and Joseph Justus, prayed, drew lots and chose Matthias. But the significant thing is that these two, along with more than a hundred others, had exactly the same qualifications. They had all walked with Jesus and remained faithful, and could all testify from their own experience that Jesus is alive.

The person chosen was Matthias. Although he had been a follower of Jesus from the beginning he had not been chosen with the original Twelve. His chance came the second time around. The second man, Joseph Justus, also a follower from the beginning, was also not chosen among the original Twelve, and missed out yet again when Matthias was preferred. The Bible tells us nothing more about either Matthias or Joseph Justus or indeed about the 100 odd others who had the same qualifications. This should be very comforting for the vast majority of ordinary Christians today who may never be chosen for any Church office, whose names may be known only to their neighbours and who go about their daily Christian witness without benefit of uniform, badge of office, clerical collar, or any other human accreditation that you are a servant of Christ. I salute you all for you have exactly the same qualification and no lesser calling as do others who are more obviously in the public eye. *That calling is first and foremost to be with Jesus.*

In today's world, *to walk with Jesus or to be with Jesus* means to be in prayerful communion and sometimes conversation with the living Jesus. Jesus is as much alive and invisible today as He was alive and visible in Palestine 2,000 years ago. We have His word that He is always available because He has said that 'where two or three are gathered together in my name, there am I in the midst'. It is impossible for a person not to grow more and more Christ-like if he or she spends more and more time with Jesus in prayer. That is why self-centred, attention-seeking people, whether priest or lay, however pious, talented, or attractive, cannot be persons of prayer. When St Paul says 'I no longer live but Christ lives in me,' he was expressing what he had come to realise; namely that being constantly in the company of Jesus it was as though he didn't know where he himself ended and where Jesus began!

On the surface the easiest form of prayer appears to be *intercession*, that is asking for help either for ourselves or for others. But it is not necessarily so. I remember some years ago when apartheid in South Africa was at its height and at its most vicious, I attended a meeting in Brent Town Hall to hear Dr Allan Boesak, the courageous anti-apartheid crusader speak. He described a situation in which a black mother trying to reach her son who had been shot by the apartheid Police was barred by a policeman with the words: 'Let the bastard die.' I found after hearing that, that when I came to pray for Desmond Tutu and others in South Africa, I had the greatest difficulty in including that policeman and others like him in my prayers. But I reminded myself that in intercessory prayer I was trying to align my will with God's will and trying to see the world through the eyes of Jesus and must therefore pray as Jesus would pray. So I could recall Jesus on the cross praying for those who were crucifying Him and saying: 'Father, forgive them – they don't know what they are doing.'

It is by tracing and retracing our steps in prayer, examining our requests to ensure that they are the kind of requests that Jesus would make, that without our own realising it, we begin to see the actions of men and women nearer to the way that God sees them. Such intercessory prayer will shade into *thanksgiving* as we begin to appreciate that sheer generosity, graciousness and mercy of God. As our prayer of *thanksgiving* follow our prayer of intercession, we begin to appreciate God's goodness in small things as well as great things. Just as Jesus said we should consider the lilies of the valley, we begin to appreciate that so much that we take for granted is really a free gift from God. That is why I never speak of 'wealth-creation', only of *'wealth-generation'*. Because to create is to form from nothing so only God can create. We human beings can use the skills He has provided, and the raw materials He has provided, and with the imagination He has given us can arrange and rearrange His gifts generating wealth in the process. But it all comes from Him in the first place, and if we are thankful for what we have, there will be no place in our hearts for envy of other people, or for the greed and ill-will that disfigure so many people's lives.

Genuine thankfulness for what God gives us will soon cause us to wonder at God's forgiving nature. Every day we see around us evidence of 'man's inhumanity to man', and how the evil that men do lives after them. Yet God's love and patience are never exhausted, and again and again He says 'I forgive'. That is the nature of the God we worship, because 'as His majesty is, so is His mercy'.

The more we ponder on God's majesty, mercy and love, it comes in on us how much He loves us even though He knows us better than we know ourselves. With Him we need no pretence, no keeping up with the Joneses. We are free to be ourselves, warts and all, secure in the knowledge that Christ will do anything for us – even die by crucifixion. All this comes about when we walk with Jesus in the prayer of intercession, the prayer of thanksgiving and the prayer of amazement. It is then that we realise that when we thought that by finding time to pray we were making our way to God, it was really God Himself all along drawing us to the warmth and light of Christ. Jesus called his disciples first that they might be with Him, so that will always be our first calling.

Secondly He called them that He might send them out. Short-sightedly we have taken this to mean primarily that we should go about talking about Jesus. Not so. We are to be carriers of Jesus. *We are witness to His Resurrection by showing that He is alive in us.* And in His parable of the sheep and goats Jesus shows how every one of us can be the means by which He continues His work. Every one of us can provide food for hungry people – if we want to; every one of us can provide clothes for those who have none – if we want to. Every one of us can provide a welcome for the stranger, the immigrant and the refugee – if we want to – and every one of us can visit sick people or people in prison if we want to. If we do not do these things it is because we do not want to do them, and those of us who are prone to spend long hours at our computers or immersed in television soaps should examine the use of our time in the light of these known concerns of Jesus.

Jesus knows well enough that if at the heart of a community there is a core of people dedicated to being with Him in prayer and carrying out the simple, practical acts of compassion which He inspires, that a whole community can be transformed. If at the heart of any nation there is such a group, that nation can be transformed, and if at the heart of our world there is such a core of people, our world will be transformed. You can be sceptical about this if you like, but you do not know for sure that Jesus is wrong! And if this is so, in a world where every night half the people go to bed hungry; where every minute of every day twenty people die of starvation or malnutrition-related diseases – the equivalent of a jumbo jet crashing and killing everyone on board every twenty minutes, where between 1945 and 1999 there were 291 major episodes of armed conflict, each episode costing at least 1000 lives, (and that was before September 11th last year and its aftermath) – and where every year the nations of the world, with millions of children without access to clean water or primary school education, prefer to spend at least 51.6 billion US dollars on guns, bombs and other weapons of destruction, can you afford not to seize the opportunity where it is just possible that action on your part may influence the situation for good? You may only be one person, but remembering the saying that anyone who thinks himself too small to be significant, has never been in bed with a mosquito!

Needless to say Christians everywhere should be part of this transforming core at the heart of the community, nation and the world, including this part of our diocese. Here in Croydon Archdeaconry you are not to wait for an invitation or a lead from church leaders of anyone else. Whether you belong to a denomination or not, whether you are a lapsed Christian or visit churches only for weddings, christenings and funerals, even if clergy and hymn singing remind you too much of the compulsory religion of your school days, Jesus still calls you to be with Him, and with Him to overcome every kind of evil with Good.

And now, my brothers and sisters in Christ, friends in this Archdeaconry of Croydon, my companions in witness and ministry these past seventeen years, in the words of St Paul to the Elders at Ephesus, 'I commend you to God and to the word of His grace which is able to build you up and give you an inheritance among all those who are sanctified… You must support the weak. And remember the words of the Lord Jesus, that He said: 'It is more blessed to give than to receive.' Keep the Faith.

21
Bishop of Southwark's Staff Meeting

Bishop's House, Streatham, London, UK
24 November 1993

A wise old Mirfield Father, Fr Lawrence Wrathall, once suggested to us students that when preparing sermons we should have on our desk a crucifix, and next to it a photograph of a typical member of the congregation. This should remind us of our task – namely to preach Christ crucified to that person. You are not a congregation, and I do not know which of you is typical, but my mandate for addressing you is in 1 Peter, chapter 5 verse 1 *I exhort the elders among you, as a fellow elder and a witness of the sufferings of Christ, as well as a partaker in the glory that is to be revealed...*

Our Gospel reading [Mark, chapter 10 verses 32-45] records one of the saddest incidents in the account of Christ's earthly ministry. For almost three years He and His twelve disciples were constant companions, always on the move, up and down the Galilean countryside. Sometimes they moved purposefully, going from one village to another; sometimes they merely meandered, not unlike the three friends in 'Last of the Summer Wine'. It was in this way that the Twelve got to know Jesus; to appreciate His view of life to hear His teachings about the Father and the Kingdom, and to observe the way He treated people.

But on this occasion there was something different. Jesus was not walking with the group or with a small knot of two or three as was His wont. They were on their way to Jerusalem, and He was out front, alone, not speaking to anyone and the disciples were afraid. They could sense that all was not well. Then He called them and explained that in a few days' time He would be handed over to the Authorities. He would be made to suffer and then hanged like a common criminal. Then came the saddest part. Immediately after the disciples had received this news about what was to happen to Jesus, they began jockeying for positions of power. The two brothers, James and John, asked Jesus for a special favour. When Christ had ushered in the New Age in which He would reign supreme, could the two of them occupy the two highest positions next to Him? Their request must have made Jesus very sad indeed.

So He had to explain – yet again. Everything He did, everything He said, was the reverse of the way values were presently ordered in the world. The New Age, His Kingdom, was not a conquest or overcoming of the world by beating the world at its own game. He was not interested in gaining mastery by having larger armies or more fire power than other people. In His kingdom *the order was reversed*. For example, in the world the perks of high office meant that *you* did not have to serve other people – you lorded it over them, you told them what to do; you made sure that things were fixed in the way you wanted them fixed. You ensured that whoever had to suffer, it was not you. But it was not so in *His* kingdom. In His kingdom, service was not a bad word. Quite the opposite, service was the criterion of pleasing God, and the quality of that service was the cost at which it was performed. The greatest person in His kingdom was really the person who served everyone else, and served them willingly. The values of the world and the values of Christ's kingdom do not merely differ in degree, they differ in kind.

Jesus-the-Servant as portrayed in this incident and teaching, is recognised and acknowledged as Lord by

Christians of all denominations and shades of churchmanship. Yet many such Christians also reject the notion of *Christian priesthood*. Servanthood yes, Priesthood no! As one of the persons currently helping women who are at present in the clearly defined servant role of 'deacon' to engage in the process of discerning a vocation to *priesthood*, it has been necessary constantly to reflect upon the essence of the priesthood.

Priesthood has to do with the offering of sacrifice. Yet because *Christian* priesthood derives from the priesthood of Jesus Christ, in which Priest and Victim are one and the same, there are twin pillars of that priesthood, together and inseparable – suffering and glory. Hence the rich biblical imagery of the Lamb and the Throne; the crown of thorns and the crown of life.

Theologians may identify the Body of Christ with the Church, and debate its boundaries – visible or invisible. But if there is *anything* on earth with which that Body can be co-terminus it must surely be with Humankind-in-suffering. It must surely be with those Latin American ghetto children who are kidnapped and have their organs removed and sold in rich European countries for transplant surgery; it must surely be with Muslim women in Bosnia and Somalia brutally and repeatedly raped by Christian men; it must surely be with the elderly African couple watching every one of their children and grandchildren die of AIDS. And unless that suffering is pointless and without value, it *has* to be sacrificial, priestly. It just has to be *in Christ*. For Christ's death brought a new valuation of suffering, linking God's use of suffering with sacrificial love. Christ was a servant but a *suffering* servant.

And the glory? Where else is the suffering of the present, and the glory of the future, held together in the 'now' of faith other than in the *Eucharist*? We who are witnesses of the suffering of Christ also behold His glory – that glory as befits the Father's only Son, full of grace and truth, and it is in the Eucharist that we see them [glory and suffering] as one. Christ is here, as we, comfortable and well fed, unworthily stand in for those who are hungry, mutilated, racked with pain – victims in the thirty-four bloody conflicts going on around the world at this time, and receive for them and for ourselves strength from His own self-giving under the forms of bread and wine. And in the midst of this suffering we also lift up our hearts in awe and join the company of heaven in a continuous hymn of wonder at the beauty of His holiness. 'Holy, holy, holy', we whisper … I for one deeply regret the omission from modern Eucharistic prayers of those words 'according to Thy Son Our Saviour Jesus Christ's holy institution' because these words make explicit that we are not merely following Christ's example, important as that is, but are also caught up in the eternity of His purpose. In the words of G. A. Studdert-Kennedy we can only marvel:

How through this Sacrament of simple things
The Great God burns His way,
I know not – He is there.

So, although you and I are never out of His presence, [for example, it goes without saying that He accompanied each one of us on our journey to this place today] it is in the *Eucharist* – this dimension – defying action of God's – that we particularly celebrate His humility and unfailing graciousness for each time answering the summons to come among us, from those He has Himself made worthy. If this be a function of priesthood, what man or woman is there among us who would not sell all to obtain this pearl of such great price?

22
Licensing of Rev'd Tim Giles

as Priest-in-Charge of St John, West Wickham, UK
23 September 1999

1 Samuel, chapter 10 verse 26
...and there went with him a band of men,
whose hearts God had touched.

These words are part of an Old Testament account of a new and exciting development in the life of God's chosen people, the Hebrews. They were getting their first king. The Lord had chosen Saul and Samuel the prophet presented him the people with the word – 'See ye him whom the Lord has chosen, that there is none like him among all the people.' He then sent them and the new king on their way, and the writer reports that there went with the new king, a band of men, whose hearts God had touched.

Tim Giles is no king. He is a humble parish priest. But we believe that at this time and in this place, he is God's choice to lead his people in this parish. How he is to do this is clearly set out in the Priests' Calling printed on the inside front cover of your service books, and I hope you will all retain your copies and from time to time read that introduction and pray for him, and for the other priests serving in the parishes of our diocese.

The purpose of a parish is to *include* people. A parish boundary is an arbitrary line on a map, but is there, not to *exclude*, but to ensure that wherever you are, you *belong*. The people in a parish may love their neighbourhood or they may dislike it: they may be settled, or they may be on the look out for a move, but because they are *there*, they are the parish. Parish means people. We must never forget that. It is significant that Tim Giles is not being instituted as a Parish Priest of St John's *Church*, but as parson of the *parish of St John's, West Wickham*.

It is often said that the Church is the family of God. This is the truth, but it is not the whole truth. The Church is that part of God's family which knows that it is part of His family. In this parish, those people who never darken the doors of any of our churches; who never say a prayer either for themselves or for anyone else; whose Sundays are spent with their cars, their boats or their gardens, these also belong to God's family – a fact which they may not know, or which they choose to ignore.

But we, who know that we are part of God's family, know that at the centre of this family is a God of love, revealed to us in the life, death and Resurrection of Jesus Christ. This God, who is the source of all being, of all beauty, light, goodness, and truth, did not wait for us to come to Him. He came to us, and in the person of Jesus Christ, entered our vulnerable human condition of pain and suffering, sin and guilt, with no thought of payment of even gratitude from us. Because of this, we now know the unearthly feeling of being loved completely, unconditionally and permanently, with a love which is not won by our goodness, our usefulness, or our success, and which can be denied us only by our refusal to accept it. Each of us occupies *first* place in a scale of values in which there is no place for social status, bank accounts, public acclaim, ancestry or any of the other value-tags which distort life on this side of the grave. It goes without saying that we want to share our knowledge of this love. This is the aim of our common witness to the world.

The priests who serve in our parishes are not only called to care for the people committed to their charge;

they are also to join with them in a common witness to the world. Since the world includes those members of God's family in these parishes who do not recognise that they are members of His family, how is this to be done?

There is a saying: 'Greater faith hath no man than the bald-headed man who buys hair restorer from a bald-headed chemist.' Your non-worshipping neighbours, as they meet you, and observe your relationships in shops, clubs, dinner parties and all the common social interchanges, must observe a quality of openness and friendship, a concern for each other's welfare; a willingness to help, an absence of condescension or envy or competitiveness, all of which add up to an irresistible winsomeness of Christian fellowship. This quality of Christian life must begin at the Lord's table, where we gather to thank God for all that He has done for us in Christ; where we receive Christ's body and blood as a foretaste of eternal life, and where we are strengthened to bear those loads which are known to him alone. So the first essential is that our worship, especially our Eucharistic worship, must be occasions of real love and fellowship and genuine communion and sharing.

This quality of Christian life and fellowship which begins at the Lord's table, should not end there. It will not be long before it bears in on us that we are in fellowship with other Christians who also gather around the Lord's table in East Timor, Northern Ireland, Sierre Leone and many other unpromising situations elsewhere, and we will want to hold them up before God continually in our prayers. Even though we cannot go in person to express our sadness at their plight, or to share with them the contents of our own food cupboards, we will want to show our concern by using our influence on their behalf with letters to MPs and newspapers, financial support to missionary societies and aid agencies, and doing all we can to remind ourselves and others that such people also belong to God's family.

For some years now, to respond to Our Lord's command to care for His people, we in this diocese of Southwark have been led to adopt the twin policies of 'shared ministry' and 'co-operative ministry' in our parishes. Shared ministry involves the partnership of clergy and lay people sharing in the pastoral and administrative work of the parish. No longer must the priest be deemed the only person to edit the parish magazine, visit sick parishioners, welcome newcomers or answer enquiries about weddings and baptisms in addition to his other tasks. Other members of the church can be trained to share these tasks and use these opportunities to proclaim the Gospel. And in co-operative ministry, the worshipping ecumenical communities in neighbouring parishes, by worshipping and witnessing together, and by pooling resources for more effective work, can strengthen and encourage in their common witness to the world.

In this respect I am pleased to say that under John Poole much has already been accomplished in this parish, and you are well on the way to an every-member ministry. In addition the thought, prayer, fund-raising and planning that have been invested in your proposed shop-front project is evidence of your concern for this neighbourhood in which you are set. You will know that our diocesan bishop makes no secret of his desire for our diocese to be on a missionary and evangelistic footing, and that every parish should play its full part in arresting the attention of the neighbourhood with the claims of Jesus.

Your new Parish Priest Tim Giles will endeavour to play his part faithfully in this enterprise in the next phase of the life of these parishes. He is a priest for whom parish ministry is both fulfilling and challenging, and he comes to us with the experience of ministry in Suffolk as well as elsewhere in this diocese. Both he and Gay his wife have known the presence of the Lord Jesus in their lives from an early age and rejoice to call Him Lord. He also knows that no one person and no one parish can know everything there is to know about the unsearchable riches in Jesus Christ; or do everything that is to be done in proclaiming Christ to the world. So he will not try to work in isolation from the other clergy and ecumenical partners in neighbouring parishes, but together with them, draw to Jesus the many restless souls in this neighbourhood who need to find their healing, reconciliation and rest in Christ. I commend Tim and Gay and their family to your love and support, and I trust that together you will form a band of men and women whose hearts God has touched.

SECTION THREE

CHRIST IN CHURCH & SOCIETY

23
Who is Jesus?

St Lawrence Church, Barbados, 21 December 2008

St Matthew, chapter 16 verses 13–15
When Jesus came into the coasts of Caesarea Philippi,
he asked his disciples, saying,
Whom do men say that I the Son of man am?
And they said, Some say that thou art John the Baptist:
some, Elias; and others, Jeremias, or one of the prophets.
He saith unto them, But whom say ye that I am?

For the past three Sundays we have been looking at the answer given by the disciples to the first of Our Lord's two questions, namely, 'Who do people say that I am?' and considering why people should have thought that Jesus was the return of John the Baptist, Elijah, or Jeremiah. This was understandable. John the Baptist, Elijah and Jeremiah had all spoken inconvenient and unpalatable truth to the people in power and suffered for it. Elijah was hunted by King Ahab and his wife Jezebel and had to go into hiding; Jeremiah was thrown into a pit and left to die; and John the Baptist was actually imprisoned and then murdered by King Herod. Jesus was also now speaking inconvenient and unpalatable truth to power, and had also been warned that Herod was out to get Him. Today we will consider in what is more a meditation than a sermon, answers to both questions.

Imagine that today, almost 2,000 years later, it is not to Peter and the other disciples that the Lord Jesus puts those questions, but to us personally as we sit here in St Lawrence Church. 'Who do people say that I am?' To the first question we may answer something like this.

Well, my grandmother told me that there is a Friend for little children above the bright blue sky, a Friend who never changes whose love will never die. Our earthly friends may fail us and change with changing years, This Friend is always worthy of that dear name He bears. She told me that you are that Friend, whose love for me will never die, and that You want me for a sunbeam. My grandmother said that is who You are.

Then my parents told me that as a child You lived with your parents in Nazareth. They said that according to the Bible, You were subject to your parents. In other words, You respected them. So You didn't tell lies to them or to anybody else, You helped with the household work and were always eager to learn. And through all your wondrous childhood You would honour and obey. Christian children all must be, mild, obedient good as You. For You are our childhood's pattern, day by day like us You grew, tears and smiles like us You knew, and You feel for our sadness, and You share in our gladness. You are a model and an example for all young people to follow. According to my parents that is who You are.

My great-aunt Catherine, my grandmother's sister, attended church almost every Sunday. She was a member of the Church Army. She told me that You were a Messiah. I thought that meant that You were related to Mr Massiah the bus driver. But she explained that You are God's Son, and God sent You into the world to save us from our sins. That is what made You the Messiah.

Later, my Sunday School teachers told me that You are a very good person who walked around with friends in Palestine. You loved people, were not scornful of anyone, and would befriend anyone, including tax-collectors, prostitutes, and even lepers. They told me that You did what You could to help sick people, blind and other handicapped people, and told interesting stories to show how people should treat one another. Stories such as the Good Samaritan, the Prodigal Son etc. You are fond of children and were annoyed when people tried to keep children away from You. But wicked people ganged up against You, got a so-called friend to tell them where to find You, and arrested You on false charges. They then got people to tell lies in court so that they could have You convicted of blasphemy against God and put You to death. After they had killed You, God brought You back to life and You are now with God Your Father. This shows that all of us who try to be good like You in this life, even if we die, will live again with God. They told me that You are the Son of God, and You still continue to help people, so if I ask God for anything in Your name, You will intercede for me, it will be granted. In other words, You intercede for us, so You are our Intercessor. That is who my Sunday School teachers said You are.

The Clergy also spoke about You. They said that there was a time when slaves were entirely owned by their masters, but their freedom from slavery could be bought if the right price was paid in full. This was called redemption. Humankind had been in slavery to sin, and therefore away from God. Because You love us, You gave Your life as the price of Humankind's redemption from sin, so You are the Redeemer. They also said that because Your suffering was painful in the extreme, both spiritually and physically, there is no pain that we can experience in this life that could be as great as Yours, so You understand everything we may have to go through in this life – illness, bereavement, betrayal, scoffing and victimization. They also said that whatever evil may threaten us now, or in the future, or at the end of time, so long as we put our faith in You, we will be saved from it. So You are the Saviour. That is Who the Clergy and others say You are.

So people have been saying that You are Friend, Example, Messiah, Intercessor, Redeemer and Saviour. That is how we may answer Our Lord's first question: Who do people say that I am? But what about His second question: Who do you say that I am?

Suppose when you return home after this service there is no one at home. You let yourself into the house, sit down and bend over to take off your shoes. When you look up, you see Our Lord standing there smiling down on you. 'Hello Jane/Jerry, [calling you by your own name]. He settles into the chair opposite, and says: 'I know who people say I am, but who do you say that I am? What am I to you? How do I fit into your life? Please tell Me at least three ways in which your knowing Me makes a difference to your life.'

Now let each of us close his or her eyes, look Our Lord Jesus in the face, and give Him truthful and honest answers to His questions, telling Him how He fits into our lives, and naming three ways in which our knowing Jesus makes a difference to our life. Let us now sit in silence for the next five minutes, and do this.

24
Christmas Eve 2005
Midnight Eucharist
St Cyprian's Church, Bridgetown, Barbados

St John, chapter 3 verse 16
For God so loved the world, that he gave his only
begotten Son, that whosoever believeth in him
should not perish, but have everlasting life.

It gets very cold in the desert at night, and the man in his little tent had made a fire to keep himself warm. The camel asked if he could put his head in for a little warmth and the man agreed. After a while the camel eased his shoulders in, then more of his body and eventually his whole body was inside the small tent. The man said: 'I don't think there's enough room for two of us.' 'Just what I was thinking,' said the camel, 'Why don't you find somewhere to go.'

In some countries around the world the Christian religion is not welcome and it can be very dangerous to be a Christian. Churches are burnt down and Christians are attacked and killed. So understandably when Christians come together, at great risk for their lives to worship, even at the great Christian festivals there is no public and ostentatious display of merriment. Instead there is a great sense of God's presence, thankfulness for His protection from the dangers that surround them daily, and deep joy and gratitude for this Faith which assures them that they are loved and valued and promises eternal life in God's presence.

On the other hand, there are countries which wear their Christian religion on their sleeve, so to speak.

Their laws, customs and traditions which shape their culture have their roots in the Christian religion, so they celebrate the Christian festivals publicly and boisterously. They even embellish the celebrations with bits and pieces that have nothing to do with the Christian faith such as chocolate eggs at Easter, and Santa Claus, Christmas trees and mistletoe at Christmas. And of course there is much eating and drinking, sometimes to excess. But these have become national cultural festivities rather than religious occasions.

Barbados is a country whose national life has been shaped by Christianity. The laws, conventions and traditions which form our culture have their roots in the Christian faith. But the modern requirements of our tourist industry that there should be all the year round merriment and spectacle of carnival, cropover, congoline, and so on are giving us a jump-up culture. For culture is not a static thing, it is more like a river whose course can be shaped by the landscape and which can gather debris and be badly polluted. So there is the danger that this non-stop jump-up, plus Santa Claus, Christmas trees and mistletoe, over-indulgent eating, drinking and luxury spending, can become a camel in the tent of our Christian culture which now says to true Christian faith 'why don't you find somewhere else to go?' I remember a television sketch which showed a man collecting his order from a liquor mart; six bottles of brandy, six bottles of whisky, six bottles of vodka, six bottles of gin, six bottles of rum, six cases of beer. As he left the shop he pulled a face and said: 'Christmas… if it weren't for the children we wouldn't bother.'

We committed Christians must not allow this to happen. It is not enough for us to sing carols at Christmas and our clergy to denounce the excesses of the population. We Christians must become more radical, that is to say we must relate to the roots of our faith. The great Christian festivals must be occasions for the clergy to teach the basics of our faith. Ranting against the ills of society is no substitute for such teaching, for what people do springs largely from what they believe and every wrong action can be traced back to some false notion of God. So at Christmas we must tell the story of Christ's birth; how Joseph the carpenter and his pregnant wife Mary could find no accommodation in a strange town and she gave birth in a stable; how ordinary shepherds going about their normal work were the first to hear from God the news that the nation had been expecting for hundreds of years; how the wise men travelled from a great distance, day and night, to find Jesus, to worship Him and to give Him gifts, and having worshipped returned to their homes another way.

We must take to heart the lessons of this story – that when we ignore the plight of those in need we may be turning our backs on Jesus; that we must not judge a person on the basis of where he or she was born; that a child born in slum or stable may yet become the winner of the Nobel Prize for Science who discovers a life-saving cure; that 2,000 years ago wise men sought Jesus and today men and women who are really wise still do. The wise men worshipped in silence and in our worship today there should be periods of silence for us to be lost in wonder at the glory and the majesty and the humility of our God; that the material gifts we bring to Christ should be the best that we can offer, and that once we have worshipped we should, like the wise men, return home by another and a better way.

That is the story we must tell. And we must go on to say that this mystery is the outward and visible expression of a profound mystical reality. A God of love, lovingly created men and women, giving them the power to love. We Humankind accepted this gift but chose to love, not God our creator, but ourselves. So everyone of us is born with this fatal tendency to think too highly of ourselves, and too little of God and other people. Now having got into this destructive pit Humankind could only sink deeper and deeper. Only God the source of all love could rescue Humankind from this predicament. He chose to do so, but He did not choose to lift Humankind from a height above as He could have done. Neither did He choose to give instructions from a distance as He could have done. Nor did He choose to protect Himself from human contamination by avoiding all contact. Instead He chose to join Humankind in his pit in order to climb with Humankind out of the pit. This would entail beginning life as every human being does – as a weak and vulnerable baby. It would entail living in truth and love all His life regardless of the suffering such integrity would bring. It would mean the seeming failure of His life's work when He died on a cross between two convicted thieves.

Two thousand years later we know that He accomplished all that He set out to do. Without taking away our right to choose He has made it possible for us human beings, born in sin, to become sons and daughters of God, and after this life to rejoice with Him in a greater light and on a farther shore. Men and women can still choose death rather than life; to love ourselves rather than God; to hurt rather than to heal. But this is the good news – that to us who receive Him, who believe in His name He has given power to become children of God, and you and I no matter how great or humble the circumstances of our birth are reborn, not of blood or of the will of the flesh, or the will of man, but of God. Thanks be to God. So we are joyful tonight with a deep and sober joy, because this mammoth achievement, this stupendous, earth-shaking, prison-opening achievement began on Christmas Day. That is the story we must tell. Theologians call it the Incarnation and the interpretation of all human life and history. Theologians speak of God's 'kenosis' or self-emptying, of his humility, of absolute power controlled by complete love. And what they mean is that God so loved the world that He gave His only Son that whoever believes in Him should not perish but have eternal life.

25
Christmas Day 2009
St Lawrence Church, Barbados

St Luke, chapter 2 verse 14
Glory to God in the highest, and on earth peace,
good will toward men.

We Christians believe in God. So do followers of Islam, Judaism, traditional African religions, Jehovah's Witnesses and many others. It is what we are celebrating on this day, Christmas Day, that sets us apart from them and from other Faiths.

Some years ago I came across an unusual and remarkable Christmas card. It depicted the Nativity scene in the stable, but apart from the animals there is no one in it but Mary, Joseph and the Baby Jesus. Mary is shown seated with the baby Jesus in the crib before her. But the light in the stable is such that the shadows of the roof-beams fall across the baby's crib – in the shape of a cross. And some distance from them Joseph is sitting on the floor in a corner, his knees drawn up under his chin and cradled in his arms, with his head slumped forward in the attitude of a very tired, puzzled man who is not at all certain that he understands what this is all about.

By revelation from God, and the benefit of hindsight, we now know what Joseph could not know then, namely that this baby son of Mary, is God, begotten of God before creation. Truly God and truly Man, two natures, divine and human in one Person. God had become human in the Person of Jesus Christ to rescue Humankind from sin and its consequences. So in celebrating the birth of Jesus we are celebrating the highlight of God's mission of Humankind's redemption, and the start of a perfect human life. This is the mystery of the Incarnation, that is, God taking human flesh, the central fact of our Christian faith and the interpretation of all human life and history.

Here is an analogy, not a perfect analogy, but still useful. Try to think of a jungle so completely dense and so completely dark that our eyes are no use to us. In such a jungle there are all sorts of dangers and pitfalls, and no trail or track to follow. That jungle is the world of sin and evil, whose darkness envelops all Humankind. One man enters that jungle, penetrates it, survives and emerges into light on the other side. In doing so he makes a trail, and now anyone who follows the way he carved out, can do the same. Human perfection is the total adherence to God's will without deviation or omission; and Jesus lived a life of perfection, and in so doing, made it possible for you and me to do the same, because as the Fourth Gospel tells us 'that to as many as received Him, to them gave He power to become sons of God.' This means that you and I, with all our human failings, can still be perfect. This is not fanciful because God is the only infallible judge of what is perfect, and since God's forgiveness is absolute and restorative, leaves no stain of sin, so when we are ransomed, healed, restored, forgiven, we are made perfect. So Christ urges us 'Be perfect, as your Father in Heaven is perfect.'

So we Christians have every reason to be excited and very happy on this 25th day of December, the date selected by the Church for our special celebration of the Incarnation in the birth of Jesus. Let every bell on earth ring out; let every church organ pour forth to the skies its melodious strain; let all the choirs in the world combine in a single, massive, joyous and note-perfect rendition of the Hallelujah Chorus, and creation would still be falling short of an adequate response to our Creator's mammoth act of love, this divine investment in human worth shown in taking human flesh. It is huge, huge, huge, beyond speech and language. To God be the glory, a great thing He has done.

We Christians must also know that God chose us for this revelation and in doing so, made us Children of the New Covenant. We must not make the mistake the Children of the Old Covenant, the Jews, made. They missed the purpose of their calling by supposing that the nations of the world were meant to serve them, the Chosen People. We also are a Chosen People, but we should know that as Children of the New Covenant our call is to serve the world by delivering to the world the message expressed in the vulnerability of that tiny infant in a stable. This message is 'Glory to God and peace and goodwill to Humankind.'

First, there is that peace from God which keeps our hearts and minds in the knowledge and love of God. It passes all understanding, and it is God's gift to those who desire to live in the Spirit of Jesus. It is an inner peace, deep within ourselves which enables us to see every other human being as someone created by God, someone for whom Christ died, and someone loved by Christ no more and no less than He loves us. In some of them Jesus may not be immediately recognised by the self-righteous and judgmental, but He is there, and those who have God's peace will see Him in them.

Secondly there is that peace on earth which begins with us and taking the form of justice, whose fruit it is, reaches out to those around us and beyond. Where there is such earthly peace there can be no hostility and violence, verbal or physical, between individuals and nations. It is such peace that will bring an end to war. But we are not there yet. In the meantime wars around the world continue to claim many thousands of lives; unnecessary poverty and avoidable diseases even more, all part of the shadow of that cross that falls across the crib of Baby Jesus.

In every society, and Barbados is no exception, there are the powerless and voiceless. These are those who are not related to the right people, or who do not know the right people, and have nothing to offer in return for favours. These are those who have legal rights in theory, but none in practice because the laws which should be their protection are not enforced. These are those who struggle to be honest and find their jobs and even their lives at risk because everyone around them is being dishonest with great profit for themselves. These are those who are condemned publicly by the 'respectable' people in daylight, and exploited by the same people under cover of darkness. When we children of the New Covenant become the voice for such voiceless out of love for the Babe of Bethlehem, we are agents of that peace on earth and goodwill that God desires for Humankind.

So today let us rejoice in the birth of our Saviour in the customary ways such as worship, giving of gifts to the Poor, hospitality for the Lonely and those away from their own families, and the retelling to children the Gospel account of the birth of Jesus. But in addition, let us also resolve that just as Jesus put His hand to the plough of our redemption and did not turn back, so we will continue to celebrate His birth by working for peace through the pursuit of justice every day of our lives, no matter how many obstacles we encounter, or setbacks we experience. To do so is to give glory to God.

26
Worship

St Lawrence Church, Barbados, 3 January 2010

St Matthew, chapter 2 verse 11
And when they were come into the house,
they saw the young child with Mary his mother,
and fell down, and worshipped him...

On Wednesday this week, the 6th January, we, the Church, will be celebrating the Feast of the Epiphany of Our Lord. It is called the 'Epiphany' which means the 'showing forth' or 'manifestation' because the Church has chosen it on which to commemorate three events in Our Lord's life that are all pointers to His identity and divinity. These events are one, the visit of the Wise Men to the Christ child; two, the baptism of the Lord Jesus by John the Baptist; and three, the first of many signs when He turned water into wine at the wedding in Cana of Galilee. It is the first of these three, the visit of the Wise Men, that receives most attention at this time, because it took place during Christ's infancy, and therefore nearest to His birth which we celebrate on 25th December. We must always remember that for us December is not the end of the Church's year, but its beginning.

We are told that when the Wise Men saw the Christ-child, they knelt and worshipped Him. All those years ago Wise Men made their way to Jesus, wise men and women still do today.

Although the Lord Jesus may choose to come to us at any time and in any place, when we are wise enough to want to visit Him, we make our way to a place like this, a church building. We come to worship, and worship is showing God how we feel about Him. Nowadays church buildings are used for many purposes, not unlike local post offices.

At a local post office we can pay utility bills, collect pensions and exchange greetings and news with friends and neighbours who happen to be there at the same time. The post office is useful for these things but it is really there for us to send and receive postal packages, and it is not a post office if we do not use it for that purpose.

Like the post office the church building can serve other purposes, but it is here first and foremost for worship. For us it is a meeting place with Christ, and we come here to worship Him, listening to Him and speaking to Him in prayer. To worship is to give expression in our speech, our silence, and our actions, to the interior sense of love, gratitude and reverence we hold for God. When we assemble here no activity, no consideration, no person must be allowed to distract us from giving God in Christ the attention and reverence in worship which are rightly His.

That is why, over the years, from Apostolic times, the Church, under the guidance of the Holy Spirit, has carefully devised Acts of Worship, which give appropriate recognition to the relationship between the Creator of all things Who has shown Himself to be a God of loving mercy, and us His creatures. The Church's liturgy has God on His throne, and keeps us in our proper place. That is why ministers who want to puff themselves up usually move away from the Church's appointed liturgy to talk about themselves.

Christ Himself provided the model when He recounted the visit of two men to the temple to pray, one a Pharisee and the other a Publican. The Pharisee stood and prayed about himself. 'God, I thank Thee that I am not as other men are. I fast twice a week; I give to the poor; I give tithes. I am not like this Publican here.' The Publican, on the other hand, bowed his head, and whispered 'God, have mercy on me, a sinner.' Commenting on this, the Lord Jesus said that it was the second man, the Publican, who went home blessed by God, having offered prayer that was acceptable to God.

So the Holy Spirit has led the Church to make the Eucharist the supreme act of worship. In the Eucharist we are following Christ's example and obeying His command. Above all, we are standing before the Father, not in our own merit and on the basis of our achievements, but with our sins forgiven through the suffering and sacrificial love of Christ our Redeemer. As the familiar hymn puts it:

> Look Father, look on His anointed face,
> And only look on us as found in Him;
> Look not on our mis-usings of Thy grace,
> Our prayer so languid and our faith so dim;
> For lo between our sins and their reward,
> We set the Passion of Thy Son, our Lord.

So it is totally out of place for any individual, man or woman, layperson, deacon, priest or bishop to try to use worship as a means of self-promotion or aggrandisement, trying to show that he or she 'is not as other men are.' That is why at the altar the priest is enveloped in long, shapeless vestments, uses the same words and carries out the same actions as any other priest. The worship is God-centred, and the devout priest will speak in a different voice of humility when he or she speaks to God in prayer from the voice of equality which he or she uses when speaking to the congregation. None of this 'Jesus, Uh love yuh' which one hears on the radio these days. This should also be reflected in the readings from the lectern. Such readings should be slow, distinct and deliberate so that every word is heard and the Holy Spirit may speak to each hearer as He sees fit. A reading of Scripture should not be a dramatic performance reflecting the individuality of the particular reader. And it should have been prepared beforehand with the reverence associated with handling holy things. There is no need for us to copy these new home-made churches by saying 'Good morning Church' instead of invoking the presence of the Holy Spirit with the traditional words 'The Lord be with you.'

And for us in the pew, no matter how familiar we are with the words of the prayers, we pray them slowly, because we are speaking to God respectfully, and newcomers should not be made to feel as outsiders because they cannot keep up with those who are racing along. I have to admit that now that I am old, when I attend funerals in some other churches I have to say the Lord's Prayer silently because I cannot keep up in what seems a race to get it over with.

In the same way we do not engage in noisy conversations while waiting for the service to begin because others may be trying to collect their thoughts about the people and matters in their lives that they want to offer up to God.

It can be said that the practice of Christianity in Barbados is rather like a fried egg. There is a centre and a large fringe, like the yolk and the white. At the centre there is a committed group of devout worshippers, regular in daily prayers and bible reading, who receive the Sacrament after proper preparation, and practice kindness to others in the community, not only their families and friends, trying their best to live in love and charity with their neighbours.

Then there is a much larger number who practice a kind of cultural folk religion. Some attend church, and some do not. Many of those who do not, will claim that they are as good Christians as anybody else because they are good people and they do not hurt anyone and they know a lot of church people who are hypocrites. In any case, they will say, Jesus did not say that you have to go to church.

We who try to accept Christ's invitation to share His Body and Blood, and assemble Sunday after Sunday to do so, do not agree with them. We believe that Christ is here in a particular way, and like the Wise Men all those years ago, we come to worship Him.

27
The Devout Life

St Lawrence Church, Barbados, 17 August 2008

Micah, chapter 6 verse 8
He hath shewed thee, O man, what is good; and what doth the LORD require of thee, but to do justly, and to love mercy, and to walk humbly with thy God?

Jesus a carpenter from Nazareth village, both irritated and frightened the proper Authorities. He irritated them because He was saying publicly that God was more like a loving father Who wanted His children to do the right thing, than a Commander-in-Chief concerned with enforcing rules. What God wanted was that men and women should love Him with all their heart, and love their neighbour as themselves. He frightened them because the common people were excited by His teaching, and followed Him in their thousands. The Authorities feared a popular uprising which would topple them from power. So they put Him to death. But He took death in His stride, and after three days rejoined His followers. On the basis of His teaching and their experience of His Resurrection, his followers, who were Jewish, accepted that He was the Christ that the Jewish people were expecting. Later they came to realize that He is the Christ for all the world, and the human face of God. Today this is the faith of the Church; this is our Faith.

The Bible testifies that in preparing the world for the coming of Christ, God had spoken to His people through His prophets, revealing aspects of His character and what are His expectations of His people. Foremost among these prophets were some who lived

700 years before Christ, such as Amos who spoke of the justice and righteousness of God, and Hosea who told of His love, mercy and forgiveness. There was also Micah who described the godly or devout life which men and women should live as their response to God's own justice, righteousness, love, mercy and forgiveness. He put it in this way: 'He has shown you O Man, what is good. And what does the Lord require of you but to do justly, to love mercy and to walk humbly with your God.' This godly or devout life is the subject of our meditation this morning.

The devout life is possible for every human being, irrespective of age, education or station in life because God's Holy Spirit supplies whatever may be lacking. For our part, only two things are necessary: First, the will. You must really want to live a godly life. No ifs and buts. You must really want to do it. Secondly, to know that you cannot do it in your own strength, but only by the grace of God. This second is called 'humility' and it is said that humility is the casket which contains all other virtues. Micah calls it 'walking humbly with God.' These are the only two prerequisites for the godly life – the will, and dependence upon God.

There are three major indispensable ingredients of the devout life. The first is persistent, individual prayer. Our Lord prayed a lot, and He taught His followers to pray. He also taught His disciples never to cease from prayer whatever the circumstances. He gave the example of the woman who had to deal with a lazy and indifferent judge, but refused to give up. In prayer we must have the persistence of that woman. So each of us must make provision in his or her life for some time to be spent exclusively with God. It must be treated as necessary to life as is sleeping or eating. It is even more important than watching 'Days Of Our Lives' or 'Judge Judy!' So the man who says that he simply cannot find time to pray is only fooling himself – he is certainly not fooling God.

In the time allocated to prayer, two elements are of greatest importance, namely thanksgiving and intercession. When we pray we should always thank God for all His blessings, including His gift to us of His Son Our Lord Jesus Christ and our Christian Faith. Let me ask each of you now to recall the year in which you were born, now the month in which you were born, and the date on which you were born. On that day there were thousands of children born in the world, and of them three out of every five died before the age of five. That you are one of the two to survive because you happened to be born in a part of the world less subject to starvation, war, floods, other natural disasters, high infant mortality and many, many diseases is entirely due to God's providence. Thank God for that and for the other blessings that flow from it, such as the loving care of parents, relatives, friends and neighbours; education, employment and your own family. Then thank God on behalf of all who do not themselves thank Him, for whatever reason such as ingratitude, lack of faith or indifference. Remember that incident in the Gospels when Jesus healed ten lepers and only one returned to thank Him? As Christians, we must be that tenth leper, thanking God on behalf of others. A heart that is full of thanks has no room for envy, jealousy or resentment of other people's gifts. A thankful heart looks on the talent of a gifted person and says 'That is not a gift God has given me, but I thank God that He has given it to her.'

And in intercession we are not trying to get things from God that would give us an advantage over people. In intercession we are trying to see the world and ourselves through the loving eyes of Jesus. He knows better than we do what is good for us, so although to the limit of our human knowledge we ask for what we consider is right, it must always be subject to His will. There is the story of an artist who had completed a painting and felt that there was nothing more he could do with it, and yet he was not satisfied with it. Then he thought he heard a voice saying: 'Put it in a circle.' He did so and everything became right. All our intercessions, all our requests to God, must be in a circle called: 'Thy will be done'.

They must also be the kind of request that Jesus Himself would make. You cannot imagine Jesus asking the Father to do anyone harm, or punish them because they have been unkind to Him, so neither should you.

The second major indispensable ingredient of the devout life is worship and witness in the Eucharist or Holy Communion service. On the night before Christ gave His life on the cross, He gathered some of His friends around Him. He reminded them that there can be no greater love than that a man should lay down his life for his friends. He then took bread and wine, gave thanks to the Father, and shared it among them. As He did so, He looked down the future ages and said to all His friends, some of us yet unborn: 'Do this in remembrance of Me'. When you and I troop through the doors of this church and present ourselves at the altar, we are answering the call of the greatest Friend of all. We cannot claim Jesus as God, Lord or Friend and spurn His invitation. That is why the Eucharist must always be Christ-centred, and must be central to our own Christian life.

The third major indispensable ingredient of a godly life is help for the world's needy. In St Matthew's Gospel, chapter 25 verse 31 and following, our Lord in the Parable of the Sheep and Goats makes it clear that religious observance on its own is not sufficiently pleasing to God. Those who are hungry and naked must be given food and clothes. Immigrants and aliens must be made welcome, housebound sick people and those in prison must be visited. The devout life involves loving the unlovely in practical ways and in the name of Christ. Nowhere does He say that they must be Barbadian!

Persistent private prayer of thanksgiving and intercession, worship and witness in the Eucharist, and help for the world's needy – these are the ingredients of a godly life. It is a life lived in the spirit of Jesus and will bear the fruit of the Spirit. We need only the will and the humility to recognise our dependence upon God. We know what God expects because He has shown us what is good: to do justly, to love mercy, and to walk humbly with Him. He will provide the strength.

28
Parenthood

There is the story of the elderly bishop whose short-term memory sometimes let him down. [Does this remind you of anyone you know?] He was fond of telling jokes in his sermons, and one day he was at a conference and heard a speaker say: 'The happiest days of my life were spent in the arms of another man's wife – my mother!' The Bishop thought that was a good one for a sermon, so the next time he was preaching, he began: 'The happiest days of my life were spent in the arms of another man's wife – Oh dear, I can't remember who she is now!'

Nonetheless for most of us, the happiest days of our lives are the days we spent in the arms of our mothers, where we were fed, protected from all danger, and all our needs were met. This was all due to our mother's love, so it is no wonder that when there was required an image from human experience to describe God's love for us, there was none better to be found in the created world than a mother's love. The People of God, through whom He makes His presence known in the world, are sometimes referred to as 'Holy Mother Church.' So the Church on Mothering Sunday, the fourth Sunday in Lent, has the twin foci of God's love for us as experienced in Holy Mother Church, and God's love for us as experienced in our relationship with our mothers.

There are four primary ways in which God's love is reflected in a mother's love. First God knew us and loved us long before we knew ourselves and were able to respond to His love. As the First Epistle of John puts it: *Herein is love, not that we loved God, but that He first loved us.* And in the book of the Prophet Jeremiah God says to the Prophet: *Before I formed thee in the belly, I knew thee.* So we Humankind made no contribution to our own creation and we were loved long before we were capable of accepting or rejecting God.

Similarly, long before a child is born, long before anyone but his mother may know that he exists, his mother knows that he is there and loves him.

Secondly, God knows that He is stronger than we are, yet He does not bully, He loves. So do mothers. The love between God and ourselves is not a love between equals. It is the love between the strong and the weak. God who is Almighty recognises that we are limited in our experience, knowledge and ability. This makes us selfish and inclined to think too highly of ourselves and too little of other people. So He is patient with us as He shows us that there are powers beyond our individual control. We cannot stop hurricanes and earthquakes and tsunamis and we would not survive for long without the help of other people. But if we share the knowledge and ability and all the other gifts which come from Him, our chances of fulfilling the purpose for which we are created, that is, to know and love Him, are that much greater.

Likewise, in the mother-child relationship, the mother is the strong one and the child is the weak one. So it falls to the mother to show the child that he is not the only person or the most important person in God's world, or even in the country, or neighbourhood or even in his own family. Brothers and sisters, neighbours and other people in the world all have their rights, and all of them contribute to his wellbeing. He must share with them and respect them. She must teach them that the time will come when they will be strong, and their parents will be weak so the responsibilities will be reversed. Children of well-to-do parents must never be allowed to think that their elderly and needy parents can be left to the mercy and pity of kindhearted neighbours, or the resources of the State, but they will automatically inherit their property because they are flesh and blood. We are all of the one flesh and blood, and those who show love should benefit, and those who are selfish should not be rewarded for their indifference.

Thirdly, God's love is sacrificial love. So is that of a good mother. The hallmark of God's love for Humankind is His Self-denial even to the point of sacrifice as seen in the life and death of Jesus Christ. The earthly life of Jesus was one long exercise of power controlled by love. Time and again He put up with insult and indignity when He could have nailed His tormentors to the spot with just one look. There was that time when James and John wanted to call down fire to consume the Samaritan villagers who were hostile to Him; there were the armed soldiers in the Garden of Gethsemane when Peter drew His sword and attacked one of the servants of the High Priest. But Christ preferred to suffer instead and to die in order to secure Humankind's freedom from sin.

A mother will deny herself every pleasure, every necessity, and even every right that is hers, for the sake of her child. There is that incident recorded in the first book of Kings, chapter 3, where two women had given birth to babies at the same time, but one baby had died, and both women claimed the live child. King Solomon called for a sword in order to cut the live baby in two so each woman could have a half. One woman agreed to this, saying: 'Let it be neither mine nor thine.' The other woman said 'Give it to her, but let the child live. I give up my claim to it.' Clearly that was the child's mother whose love for her child was greater than her insistence on her rights.

Fourthly, God wants us to be responsible and accountable. So should mothers. With God, over-indulgence is not the same as love, and no substitute for it. Neither should it be with a good mother. Jesus taught that there is such a thing as accountability. In the parable of Dives and Lazarus, Dives enjoyed all the riches, luxury and everything that money could buy in this life, and he chose to ignore the poverty and suffering of the poor man Lazarus. As will happen to all human beings, rich and poor alike, they both died, and in the hereafter they found their situations reversed. The rich Dives pleaded in vain for relief from the unbearable suffering he was now experiencing. Christ also told the parable of the Day of Judgement when everyone would be called to account for the selfish or unselfish way they had lived.

So it is incumbent upon the good mother to teach the growing child that words and actions have consequences, both in this life and in the life to come. There are some phrases that are in common usage that should never fall from the lips of Christians and the good mother will see to it that her children never use them. Phrases such as 'I don't care' and 'That's your problem' and 'I am good to those who are good to me' and 'I couldn't care less about them. They don't give me anything' and 'I please myself, I don't care what anybody thinks' and 'What I do, I do for me.' And so on. The mother who says: I am for 'my children, right or wrong' is a bad mother. That is to encourage children to believe that they are accountable to neither God nor Man.

Finally, in some cultures the care and upbringing of the children are exclusively the responsibility of mothers until boys are old enough to accompany their fathers to hunt, fish, tend cattle or fight. But increasingly in modern society it is accepted that fathers should play a more active part in the nurture of children, both girls and boys. Perhaps in due course 'Mothering Sunday' will become 'Parenting Sunday' and it will be a great day when both mother and father can say with pride to all their children: 'You are becoming more and more like your Father – in heaven!'

29
The Active Life

Jeremiah, chapter 31 verse 3
...I have loved thee with an everlasting love...

If you have ever witnessed the construction of a building strong enough to withstand the fury of hurricanes and the convulsions of earthquakes, you will notice that first there is a digging down through fertile soil, then there is laid a solid bed of concrete and steel, and it is on this solid bed that first, the foundations, and then the remainder of the building are constructed. Without this solid bed of concrete and steel, the building, whatever its appearance, remains vulnerable to the elements.

Around this time of year, we preachers are to be heard lamenting that the goodwill and generosity so much in evidence at Christmas are not maintained throughout the coming year. We lament this with a kind of resignation as though this is how it has always been, and how it will always be, because people cannot sustain good intentions and good actions towards others for any length of time. But we must not accept this. Instead we must say, 'Yes, we can. We are Christians.'

There is such a thing as the active Christian life. What is more, every one of us is called to it, young and old, men and women, rich and poor. It is not for the clergy and a few special people only. Every one of us in this building today is called to the active Christian life, and such a life is like a building. Some of it is above ground and is easily seen, and some of it is hidden from view.

The solid bed of concrete and steel on which the active Christian life is built, is our love for God. There are many reasons for our loving God, but the overriding reason for our loving God is that He first loved us, loves us, has always loved us, and will never stop loving us. He has said to us: I have loved you with an everlasting love. That is why we do not have to be in church, or on our knees, or at any particular time of the day, for us to say: 'God our Father, I love You because You loved us first, and will never stop loving us.' If you drive to work each day, you can make a point, whenever you reach a particular place, a junction, or traffic lights, or a building, to say to God, 'God, our Father, I love You because You first loved us, and because You will never stop loving us.' When you go to make the beds, or switch on the washing machine, or open the windows for the first time each day, you can say, 'God, our Father, I love You because You first loved us and You will never stop loving us.' Let a particular action or sight remind you of how much you love God, and when it does, tell God that you do.

Although the overriding reason for our loving God is that He first loved us and will never stop loving us, there are specific attributes and actions on God's part that cause us to be reminded of this. For example, there is His goodness in creating this universe and us in it. God did not need to create the Universe. God needed nothing, because within the Godhead of the Trinity of Persons there is the all-sufficiency of love. Yet He chose, in His goodness to create us as a work of love.

Then there is God's generosity, seen all around us, but seen particularly in the gift of His Son Jesus Christ our Lord, whose life showed us how to live, whose death redeemed us from sin, and whose Resurrection assures us of eternal life. Whenever we think of such generosity, we are moved to say: 'God our Father, I love

You because You first loved us and You will always love us.'

Then there is God's grace and mercy. With the best will in the world, and despite our best endeavours, from time to time we fall into sin, committing acts we know are not pleasing to God. And yet when we turn to Him in sorrow for our failures, He always forgives. And He does not do so grudgingly, but forgives us with graciousness. He wants us to turn from our wickedness. That is why in the confessional, the final words from the priest to the penitent are gentle and gracious words: 'Go in peace. The Lord has put away all your sins. And pray for me, a sinner also.' It echoes Our Lord's gracious words to the woman taken in adultery: Neither do I condemn thee. Go and sin no more. Well may we pray: God our Father, I love You because You first loved us and will always love us.

That is the kind of bedrock of our love for God on which our active Christian life is built which will ensure that goodwill and generosity are permanent features of our relationships with others.

But what about the active Christian life itself? It has three discernible features, which, like a building, may be seen by other people. The first of these is prayer and meditation. Because we now live in such a noisy, busy environment and prayers are no longer an automatic feature of our working lives such as in schools or colleges, we must make our own time for a moment of quiet with God. It could be out walking in the morning, or on the beach, or on the exercise bike or treadmill, or in the garden. Such prayer time must be fed by reading episodes from the Gospels featuring the actions or words of the Lord Jesus, and sharing His concern for all His children including those you have never met or are likely to meet, such as those in the war-torn areas of the world such as Palestine, Iraq, Sri Lanka and elsewhere. Pray for the witness of the Church and its leaders in its mission to infect the world with righteousness. In places where the Church is persecuted pray for courageous leadership to strengthen and encourage the Faithful; in the rich and affluent parts of the world pray that its leaders may not be silent or seduced into collusion with corruption.

The second feature of the active Christian life is Public Worship. From earliest times men and women of faith have come together to address God in thanks and praise, penitence and supplication. We Christians continue to do this. Our public worship takes a particular form following the example and command of the Lord Jesus. On the night before He gave His life for us, with His friends around Him, He took bread, gave thanks to the Father, broke the bread and shared it among them. He then took a cup of wine, gave thanks and gave it to them, asking them, whenever they ate that bread or drank that cup, to do it in remembrance of Him. So this observance is an indispensable part of an active Christian life.

The third indispensable feature of the active Christian life is the practice of good works, and these must include those known as the Seven Corporate Acts of Mercy. These are:

1. Giving food to those who are hungry,
2. Giving drink to those who are thirsty,
3. Giving clothes to those who are naked,
4. Giving shelter to those who are strangers and without homes,
5. Visiting those who are sick,
6. Visiting those who are in prison, and
7. Burying the dead.

The first six of these good works are listed in Our Lord's parable of the sheep and goats in St Matthew's Gospel, chapter 25 from verse 31 onwards.

So it is possible, by living the active Christian life to which we are called, to maintain the Christmas goodwill and generosity all the year round. It must be rooted in our love for God who loved us first, who loves us with an unchanging love, and who will never stop loving us. So we make a point of saying to Him: God our Father, I love You because You first loved us, and will never stop loving us.

To sum up: there are three elements, that is, prayer including meditation, public worship centred on the Eucharist, and the practice of good works which must include feeding the hungry and thirsty, clothing the naked, providing shelter for the stranger, visiting those who are sick, visiting those in prison, and burying the dead. Our love for God should give us the will to do these things. His love for us will give us the strength.

30
The Cross of Jesus

Holy Week, Bishop's Staff Meeting address
Bishop's House, Streatham, London, 10 April 1990

In a culture such as ours where moderation is regarded as the greatest of all virtues, and extremism the greatest of all vices, Jesus on the cross is a stumbling block. Everything about the death of Jesus is extreme. There is a miscarriage of justice when an innocent person is mistakenly convicted. It is *extreme* injustice when the innocent is convicted, not by *mistake* but deliberately; and punished, not with loss of liberty or property but with the *finality of death*. Even that and death by torture is made more extreme still when it is public so that the death-throes of the victim provide entertainment for onlookers. When in addition to all this we consider that only the spiritually mature can feel the full weight of moral evil, it is no wonder that gritted teeth could not altogether choke the accusatory cry: 'My God, my God, why hast Thou forsaken Me?' To accuse the Father, who can never be other than true to Himself, of deserting His beloved Son – that is extremism indeed.

The cross was, for Jesus, the extreme price of extreme commitment. He was totally committed to what He described as the 'Kingdom of Heaven'. For Him this kingdom was realisable on earth, and its realisation was somehow dependent upon a convergence of God's will and the will of Humankind. How else can we explain the very first intercession in the prayer He taught His followers, namely 'Thy kingdom come, Thy will be done on earth as it is in heaven'? Jesus ate, slept and breathed this kingdom – His teaching, His healing,

His power were all signs of the kingdom, and He missed no opportunity of inviting His hearers to step out of *their* reality into His. His reality was something that His hearers could comprehend but not accept – so far was it from their experience and their expectation. If He was to be believed in this kingdom men and women would all be of equal worth; ties of blood, of kith and kin would be subordinate to the higher good of doing the will of the Father; riches, as an encumbrance would be disposed of; the lame would walk, the dumb speak and the poor would receive good news. Worship would be in spirit and in truth. He was not pleading for favourable consideration of a new experimental life-style. He was claiming that this was God's way and therefore the only valid way.

He knew that this meant an overturning of the established order so he could not have been surprised that the Civil Powers and the Religious Authorities would be aligned against Him and would seek to silence Him. Since He knew nothing of compromise and owed no allegiance to the god moderation, the path He was treading could only end at Calvary. It did.

Is there anything that you and I would gladly suffer and die for today? Hardly, I think [speaking for myself]. The idealising of moderation and compromise means that suffering can be described as self-inflicted since it could have been avoided and holding on to our convictions can sometimes transform us into persons with whom it is too dangerous to be identified. When our convictions run contrary to the status quo, of the majority opinion, or the wishes of the powerful, people quickly come to see that we spell trouble. The disciples ran away from Jesus because He was beginning to smell of death. It was better and safer to be in the crowd where no one could identify them or victimise them.

Some years ago when discussing the American Civil Rights Movement, a reporter asked the then Archbishop of Canterbury, Dr Coggan, if he shouldn't be playing in this country the role that Martin Luther King had played in the USA. Dr Coggan, a humble man in spite of his undoubted ability and achievements, replied [I believe sincerely] that he was not quite in that league. I remember thinking at the time that with respect that was not the whole truth. Rather that the managers of the church are expected to manage it within the parameters of convention and law in this country, and this did not include respectable church leaders leading demonstrations!

We respectable church leaders need to remind ourselves that if it was human sin that brought Jesus to the cross, it was the *respectable* people who crucified Him – the people of their traditions. Yet to them this was simplistic, unsophisticated and with dangerous rabble-rousing potential. Better that one man should die than the whole nation perish. He continues to ask this, but you and I know that although from a safe distance we may profess admiration for an Archbishop Romero or a Martin Luther King or a Desmond Tutu, what is expected of us are the management skills which ensure that compromise and moderation triumph over any unseemly extremism – even the extremism of love which ends in sacrifice.

Let us conclude with St Augustine's meditation on the crucifix.

Look thou upon the wounds of Him who hangeth
The blood of Him who dieth,
The price paid by Him who redeemeth thee
His head is bent to kiss
His arms set wide to embrace
His heart laid open to love

His whole body laid out to redeem
Think thou what great things are these.
Weigh them in the balance of thy heart
That He may be fixed whole in thy heart,
Who for thy sake was fixed whole upon the tree.

31
Low Sunday 2008

St Lawrence Church, Barbados, 30 March 2008

1 Corinthians, chapter 15 verse 19
If in this life only we have hope in Christ, we are of all
men most miserable.

In the diocese of Southwark in the UK there are three prisons: Brixton Prison, Belmarsh Prison and Wandsworth Prison. Every Christmas Day and Easter Day, the Bishops of the diocese celebrate the Eucharist in all the prisons. One Easter day I was celebrating the Eucharist in Wandsworth Prison and began my sermon by saying 'St Paul says that in this life there are three things that will endure. Faith and Love are two. Can you name the third?' One inmate raised his hand and called out: 'I know – Wandsworth Prison!' It was not the answer I was expecting!

The answer I was looking for was of course 'Hope' because our Festival of Easter when we celebrate the glorious Resurrection from the dead of Our Blessed Lord, is pre-eminently the Festival of hope.

For three years the young charismatic teacher and healer from Nazareth named Jesus had been teaching that God is a loving Father, and not a tyrannical judgemental ruler, speaking to crowds in their thousands, smaller groups in homes, and to individuals, He had so inspired His hearers that many had become convinced that the day was near when their nation would be restored to its former glory, and that Jesus was the person who would lead the revolution. So at the great Passover Festival when Jerusalem was crowded with people from all over the country there was a great air of expectancy. The people were ready; would Jesus make His move? The rulers took fright, waited until everyone was indoors for the night observing the Passover meal customs, arrested Him, put Him through a mockery of a trial, crucified Him, quickly took His body down from the cross and buried Him, thinking that would be the end of Him.

His close followers who knew what happened, were devastated. They too had hoped that He was the person to restore Israel to its rightful place as the leader of nations. And now all these hopes had come to nothing. Years of excitement, wonder, teaching and good works had ended in a grave.

In Holy Week and Easter each year, the Liturgy of the Church is designed to help us believers to experience a little of the sorrow and deep emotions of the disciples at that time. So the Maundy Thursday Eucharist recalls that last Passover Supper with Christ: the stripping of the altar depicts the humiliation of Christ as He is dragged from pillar to post, stripped of His own clothes, given imitation royal attire and mocked before finally being flogged and nailed to the cross.

Even so it is difficult for us to imagine the feelings of despair and hopelessness that engulfed those disciples on that Friday and Saturday. On the Sunday afternoon two of them were walking to a village called Emmaus when a third man joined them and asked why they were so sad. So they told him about Jesus and how He had been put to death. They were sad, they said, because they had hoped that He was the person who was going to save their nation. But now this hope had come to nothing. The stranger explained to them that they had been reading the scriptures in the wrong way. It was all there in the scriptures, but they had been so caught up in the idea of political power, and military power, and economic power, that they could not see past this kind of power to the kind of power in which God is most clearly seen. That power is Sacrificial Love, and the Crucifixion of Jesus, rather than defeat, was victory achieved through this kind of power, and His Resurrection was witness to this.

Their hearts burned within them as He opened the scriptures to them in this way, and they invited Him to have supper with them. As He took the bread, gave thanks and broke it, they recognised that it was Jesus. He was alive. They hurried back to Jerusalem to give the other disciples the news, and the others confirmed that they too had seen the Risen Lord!

You and I cannot imagine the joy of the disciples. The nearest we can get is to think of a five-day test match between the West Indies and Australia in Australia. The West Indies had been given 500 runs to make to win, and at the end of the fourth day's play had scored 200 for the loss of nine wickets. Fidel Edwards and Cory Collymore were the last two men at the wicket. We went to bed and woke up next morning to hear that Edwards and Collymore had not only survived, but had knocked off the 300 runs and West Indies had won the match!

Sadly, even some of the disciples still did not grasp the true significance of Our Lord's Resurrection, and continued to think of worldly power. Remember how they asked Him if He would be restoring the Kingdom to Israel, and if the two Zebedee brothers could sit on His right and left?

We Christians of today are grateful for the biblical record and the testimonies of the disciples who recognised the Risen Lord as the teacher with whom they had shared so many experiences. But even without such testimonies our knowledge of the Resurrection is attested by our own experience of the living Christ in our own lives. Some of us have heard His voice speaking to us at various stages of our lives; some of us, looking back, have recognised how He has guided our footsteps past many dangers and pitfalls; others in moments of near-despair, have been strengthened by His assurance: 'Be of good cheer, I have overcome the world.' All of us, I dare to say, are aware of His abiding presence.

For us therefore, the first day of every week, the day of the discovery of the empty tomb and the first appearance of the Risen Lord, is our day of celebrating Our Lord's Resurrection so it is on this day we assemble at His request to partake of His Body and Blood as pledges of the new life to come. But once a year, at Easter, this Queen of Festivals, we adorn our celebration with extra festivities. But far more important is that in our daily lives should be reflected the love and graciousness of persons who know ourselves to have been redeemed from sin and evil by Christ's sacrificial death, and that His Resurrection proves that this is so.

32
Whitsun 2004

Whitsunday
St Cyprian's Church, Barbados, 30 May 2004

St John, chapter 14 verse 15-16 Jesus said:
If ye love me, keep my commandments.
And I will pray the Father, and he shall give you another
Comforter, that he may abide with you for ever;

Three fundamental truths must be constantly in our minds.

First, that the Gospel or Good News is exactly the same today as it was the moment Jesus was born, and will be the same to the end of the ages. The Gospel needs no addition or diminution, and will never, never change. The Gospel is that God is, in Jesus Christ, reconciling the world to Himself, not counting our misdeeds against us. That is the Gospel and it will never change.

Secondly, the primary means, the first and foremost means of communicating the Gospel, like the Gospel itself, will never change. The question is: what is that primary means?

Thirdly, there are other means of communicating the Gospel which can change from time to time – indeed *must* change. These are secondary means, and will be influenced by contexts, cultures and civilisations. These secondary means of communicating the Gospel include books about God, including the Bible, music, preaching, radio broadcasts, drama, film and television. These means can be very effective, but they are also open to misunderstanding and misuse, and may convey, not the Gospel in its entirety, but those features of the Gospel that are of passing attraction to a particular generation at a particular time. So they are essentially a secondary means of communicating the Good News of Jesus Christ. But the first and foremost means of communicating the Gospel is represented by the event which the Church commemorates today, Whitsunday.

You know the facts. After the Crucifixion, Resurrection and Ascension of Jesus, the twelve disciples had assembled on the Jewish festival of Pentecost, when suddenly in the room there was the sound of a forceful wind like a hurricane, and the brightness of fire above each person's head. They began to speak and found themselves speaking various foreign languages. As they went out into the street, people from various parts of the world heard in their own languages, the good news of Jesus Christ. Many believed and were baptised. The Christian Church had been born with a bang!

Those are the facts, but it is helpful to know the background.

Approximately 2,000 years ago the Hebrew nation, although colonised and ruled by the Roman Empire still clung to the conviction that the day was coming when they would once again be the leader of the nations of the world. Since it was military might and a strong central leader that ruled the world, they kept their eyes on the distant horizon looking for their own strong saviour leader to come galloping over the horizon and call them to arms.

So understandably they were not inclined to listen to a home-grown, lowly-born village carpenter–turned-wandering-preacher named Jesus who was suggesting that this hope was mistaken and that there was another way. As far as they were concerned He was just an irritant, and when the irritant became a thorn in the flesh, the Authorities just got rid of Him by judicial capital punishment, which at that time took the form of crucifixion.

But before they got around to killing Him, Jesus had made a tremendous impression upon those who had come into contact with Him – ranging from the prostitute Mary Magdalene to the parliamentarian Nicodemus. His own way of life was plain for all to see and it was certainly different from that of the majority of people around him. His spoken or unspoken invitation – challenge, if you like – to all and sundry was for them to step out of their reality, and into His; to exchange their way of life for His. His very existence was a call to faith. This invitation was taken up by twelve men in particular and there came about between them and Jesus, a relationship which emanated from *His presence* and gave *them* a certain kind of strength.

Those twelve men, who experienced that peculiar intimacy with Jesus, saw him crucified and buried and knew the loss of that relationship. When days later they found themselves again walking and talking with Him, and once again experiencing that same relationship, that strange strength coursing through their very being they knew that this was no ghost, this was the same Jesus. Clearly He is stronger than anything in this world, including death itself.

Now although it was as *individuals* that each of these twelve had stepped out of their reality into that of Jesus, they walked with Jesus and followed Him as a *group*. Now, as a group they witnessed to His Resurrection, many others joined them to follow the way of Jesus.

In our modern craving for the spectacular and the bizarre, people are drawn to the phenomenon of speaking foreign languages without having to learn them, and receiving supernatural power to put on eye-catching performances. But just as Jesus did not give in to the Devil's temptation to do something spectacular to get people to believe in Him – such as throwing Himself down a precipice or turning stones into bread, the Holy Spirit was not given in order for the disciples to dazzle other people or to show off. The Holy Spirit is none other than the Spirit of Jesus, so He is all powerful, His power is the servant of love. He came to transform the disciples into apostles; to make the fellowship of believers into a missionary community. Its mission is the mission of Jesus – the agent through whom God reconciles Humankind to Himself, not holding our misdeeds against us.

So we must love one another as Jesus loves us. By this all will know who we are, and for this – to love one another as Jesus loves us, we are given the supernatural power of the Holy Spirit. That is why the Holy Spirit is given to the Church; that is why the love of Christ in the Church draws men and women like a magnet. When we love one another as Christ loves us, we are preaching Christ. We need no gimmicks or play acting to impress gullible people. That is what St Francis meant when he said: 'Preach Christ at all times – use words if necessary.' *The primary, first and foremost means of communicating the Gospel to unbelievers, to new generations, to people of other faiths and of winning souls for Christ,* is a Church that is a community of love. The Holy Spirit is not some kind of magic ingredient in certain individuals. He is the Spirit of Jesus at work among His people. It has been that way from that first Whitsun, it is so today, and will be until end of the Age. Bible-thumping, paid missionaries, evangelistic crusades, all have their place, but none can be a substitute for a church where everyone sees his or her neighbour through the eyes of Jesus, and loves him as Jesus loves him. As the Apostle John says: 'We *know* that we have passed from death to life – because we love the brethren'.

What meaning has all this for us in the year 2004 here in the parish church of St Cyprian's, Barbados? Are we people who 'go to church at St Cyprian's' or are we true followers of the Way? Have we as a group of believers received the Holy Spirit, and can His presence be recognised because we form a community of love? In Galatians, chapter 5 verse 22 the writer describes the fruit or marks of the Spirit as love, joy, peace; patience, kindness, goodness; faithfulness, gentleness and self-control. You will notice that these all have to do with human relationships, no mention of falling over backwards, or shouting out or any other attention-seeking activity. It is only the Holy Spirit that can make a church a Community of love, because only the Holy Spirit can empower one person to go up to another church member and say: 'I have come to ask you to forgive me for what I said about you, or said to you.' Only the Holy Spirit can empower that other person to reply: 'Thank you for asking my forgiveness. I am glad to give it, because we are all sinners and Christ loves both of us. Please pray for me.' Only the Holy Spirit can help us to mean what we say when we pray: 'Forgive us our trespasses as we forgive those who trespass against us.' Only the Holy Spirit can help us to do unto others as we would have them do unto us. Only the Holy Spirit can help us to find happiness in other people's happiness so that we genuinely do rejoice with them that do rejoice and weep with them that weep. Only the Holy Spirit can give you the courage to say gently to the person spreading malicious gossip: Would you like that to be said of you by another church-member? It is not natural to do any of these things, but life in the Spirit is a supernatural life.

As you know, another name for the Holy Spirit is the

Comforter. To comfort someone is to give the person encouragement, and occasionally encouragement is painful. In Bayeux in France there is the famous tapestry depicting the 1066 Battle of Hastings. It shows King William prodding one of his soldiers from behind with his spear. The caption reads: 'King William comforts his troops!' The Comforter can encourage us followers of the Way by many different means, and because we do not always want to do what is right, He will sometimes have to prod us, perhaps somewhat painfully.

33
Inner Life

St Lawrence Church, Barbados, 5 July 2009

St Mark, chapter 6 verse 4
But Jesus, said unto them,
A prophet is not without honour, but in his own country,
and among his own kin, and in his own house.

Hundreds of years ago, here in Barbados, Sir Christopher Codrington, in his will, made provision for the establishment of a college where medical doctors and ministers of religion could be trained at the same time so that men's souls and bodies would both be cared for. In this he was reflecting a fundamental and long-established Christian understanding that every person has a physical life and an inner life. Another name for the inner life is the life of prayer, because it is in the inner life that we are either in communion with God our Maker or we are not. Communion with God is called prayer.

Sir Christopher recognised that just as if a person's physical life is to develop in good health, fight off ailments and disease, it has to be nurtured and cared for in the right way, the same is true for the inner life or the life of prayer. Neither will prosper without care, and both will suffer from neglect.

The physical life is a visible life. Other people can see and we ourselves can feel when we have wounds that bleed, disorders that lead to swellings, or when we are handicapped by blindness, deafness, loss of limbs or other handicaps which stunt or restrict our physical life. Indeed, persons with handicaps know only too well how irritating it is to be told repeatedly what they already know, such as people saying to an amputee: 'You have lost a leg!' So there is no way we can be ignorant of defects in our physical life. If we try to ignore them, other people are sure to remind us!

But the inner life is not a visible life. We can no more see the communion between God and ourselves than we can see the airwaves through which telephone calls between Barbados and Australia pass. But the inner life is just as real as the physical life, and just as subject to its own ailments, disease and neglect as the physical life. Indeed, Christ says that it is not what is outside a man that defiles him, but what comes from inside, because that is where evil thoughts, wickedness, deceit, theft, murder etc. begin in the heart. God knows when that inner life is sick, and sometimes discerning folk recognise the symptoms as well.

To help us, God chooses certain people and endows them with gifts of discernment, and with courage to speak bravely to us about our shortcomings. Such people are called prophets. The thermometer the prophet uses to measure our inner life or life of prayer, is the known will of God. He knows that God has already provided us with all that is necessary for inner health, namely salvation through the life, death and Resurrection of His Son, and our conscience through which God speaks to us. All we have to do is to love Christ as He loves us, and to obey our conscience. Other discerning people may also conclude from observing our behaviour that our inner life is not aligned with God's will, but God lays it upon the prophet to speak to us about it.

In today's Gospel reading, Our Lord pays tribute to prophets. He says that no prophet is without honour. But then He adds, 'except among his own people.' Christ knows that many persons may appear physically well but sick in their inner life so they cannot be healthy in the true sense. He knows also that such people are often ignoring their conscience, and closing their eyes to God's love and the demands it makes upon them in preference for impressing those who envy and admire them for their wealth and power. In other words they are fooling the public while killing their own consciences and rejecting Christ. They have no time for anyone who will ask them awkward questions or force them to think seriously about Christ. Their immediate reaction is to try to discredit the prophet in order to tell themselves that they need pay no attention. So they claim that the prophet has not got their own better education, background, or achieved as much as they have, or command the influence they do, so he is a loser they can ignore.

Sir Christopher's vision was only partly realised because it was not found practicable to train medical doctors at the College in St John. But Ministers of Religion, mainly Anglican priests, have been trained there for generations. They are meant to be carers for our inner life or life of prayer, persons to whom we turn when we are finding communication with God difficult, when we are troubled by bad consciences, when we are having to hold on to our faith in God's love for us by our finger-tips. That is why clergy must first and foremost be persons of prayer. Otherwise it will be a case of 'Physician, heal thyself!' They are not meant to be friendly menials, paid to take weddings and conduct funerals. They are to be doctors of the soul, watching over our inner life, and warning us when pride, self-importance and hypocrisy are crippling our inner life. In other words, they are also called to be prophets.

In Barbados religion now seems a mere cultural feature, on the leisure and entertainment fringe of community life. So it becomes easy for some clergy to accept the role of entertaining preachers, who make us laugh, who are said to be 'down to earth', which is another way of saying that they can sometimes be rather crude. It is this descent into vulgarity that is marked by some people in our Anglican churches clapping at the end of sermons. The other churches know better than this and may say 'Amen' or 'Praise the Lord.' Where in the Gospels do we read that people clapped after hearing Jesus speak? On the contrary in St Luke's version of this incident from which our text is taken, the people tried to kill Him. Please God this mindless desire for entertainment in the name of religion will never come to St Lawrence, and for some folk a high point of their week will remain the half-hour of silent prayer before the Eucharist begins, second only to receiving Christ in the Holy Sacrament.

Our inner life grows by feeding on Christ in three specific ways. First, because we want to know Him better and better and love Him more and more, we must read the Gospels of Matthew, Mark, Luke and John constantly and prayerfully. We must give ourselves time when we read, to sit and think about what Christ said and did in the various incidents, and imagine Him speaking the words to us. Also, because Christ is alive it may be that He may choose to speak to us at these times when we have chosen to listen to Him.

Secondly, we must find time to pray. When we pray, we must think of Christ welcoming us and those we have brought with us into His presence. So we bring, not only those who are nearest and dearest to us, but those less fortunate than ourselves, and whose needs are greater than our own. These will include those who are so dear to Our Lord's heart, such as those who find themselves hungry and thirsty, naked, strangers in a strange land as exiles, refugees, immigrants or homeless; those who are sick and those in prison, particularly those who have been unjustly convicted. We must pray for them all.

It is a good practice, when you take down your Christmas cards after Christmas, to keep them, and each day pray for one or more of the persons who have sent them. It is also a good practice when you close your newspaper after reading it, to pray for the people you have read about, asking God, whatever their circumstances, to send them the help that will guide them to Him to know the love of Christ. Another good practice is to use the days of the month and the letters of the alphabet to pray for those you know. For example, on the first those whose surnames begin with the letter A; on the second, B; on the third C etc. And please remember to pray for those you consider to be your enemies or detractors. You should ask God that if there is in you any fault that rightly causes offence, that He should remove it, but if they dislike you without any fault on your part, He should forgive them and restore them to love.

The third way is to share in the Sunday celebration of Our Lord's Resurrection and receiving His Body and Blood under the forms of bread and wine.

In helping you to nourish your life of prayer, the priest-prophet will sometimes have to tell you things you do not want to hear. In other words, he or she will challenge your conscience. Your conscience must be educated and respected. Individual conscience plays a vital part in public morality both personally and as the community. For example, it is not difficult to see that in a society where self-pleasing, not morality, is what matters, children will decide that what is good for the goose is good for the gander, and choose to please themselves with no more and no less morality than their parents do.

With such a state of affairs, our priests, although knowing that among our own people they may not be held in honour for their prophetic utterances, they must call us to repentance, so that in God's name they can absolve and declare the forgiveness of sin. In this way our inner life will remain healthy, and others, taking note, will glorify God.

34
Accountability

St Lawrence Church, Barbados, 5 October 2008

St Matthew, chapter 21 verse 37
...They will reverence my son.

Every parable from the mouth of Our Lord provides much food for thought and many points on which to ponder. But always there is one central point of teaching which the Lord Jesus is concerned to communicate to his hearers. The parable in today's Gospel found in Matthew, chapter 21, is no exception. A landowner enters into a partnership agreement with some men who were to farm the land, and share the produce with him. But when he sent a servant to collect his share of the produce, the men beat him and chased him away. The landowner sent another servant and they stoned him. The landowner sent yet another servant and this time the men beat him and then killed him. The patient landowner decided to send his own son in the hope that the men would respect him, but he was wrong. The greedy men thought that if they killed the son there would be no one to inherit the land and they could have the whole lot for themselves. So they murdered the son. The landowner was forced to take action against them and destroy them.

In meditating on this parable we may consider how greed, once it gets hold of you, can drive you to extreme actions which normally you would not dream of taking. We can think of brothers and sisters who normally get on well together are suddenly at each other's throats over property left by deceased relatives, leading to murder, either in the heat of argument or premeditated. Or we can think of the long-suffering forbearance of the landowner who clearly believed in giving people a second chance even at cost to himself. Or we can reflect that we can push our luck too far, and bring about our own destruction. There is also the shameful and dishonourable breaking of promises and agreements. We might consider that Jesus may even have been predicting His own death. These are all there in the parable. But none of these is the central point of Our Lord's teaching.

The central point of Our Lord's teaching is that there are people who accept partnership with God with accountability to Him and then betray His trust. The Lord Jesus knew that in the crowd listening to Him were some of the political and religious leaders of the nation. He also knew that they knew that He was speaking to them. They knew that the landowner in the story was God, and the property was God's people, the nation of Israel. The servants who had been sent were God's prophets. Prophets like Jeremiah who was thrown into a pit, Micaiah who was imprisoned, and like John the Baptist who was beheaded, all of whom had spoken in the name of God to those in power. These national leaders heard Jesus, did not like what they heard, and crucified Him.

In our day there are three levels on which we are involved in accepting partnership with God and accountable to Him. On the individual level, some of us accept at God's hand the awesome responsibility of being parents. We accept responsibility for the future of the human race. But we betray that trust when we use children for our own ends by neglecting their welfare while we pursue our own interests and greed, and in extreme cases abuse them physically and sexually. Fathers who leave children and wives to fend for themselves, and mothers who abandon their children to the care of whatever woman the fathers can lay their hands on, are betraying God's trust.

On the international and national levels, political leaders go to enormous lengths to get into positions of authority, often invoking the name and blessing of God. For example, in the current American presidential election campaign, nearly every speech ends with: 'God bless you, and God bless America.' This was also done in previous elections, but as subsequent events demonstrated, the leaders contrived to become richer and richer, while the poor became even poorer. And this has been the pattern in many nations around the world. Sadly, we seem resigned to this. Politicians and holders of public office who frequent church services and other such occasions, but make decisions governed by their chances of personal enrichment, are people who have entered into partnership with God, with accountability to Him, but have betrayed His trust.

But it is on the third level that accepting God's offer of responsibility and then betraying trust is most disastrous. Human sin and estrangement from God proved so destructive of the proper relationship between God and His creation, that only the willing sacrifice of the life of the Son of God, dying painfully on a cross could restore this and re-open Humankind's way to God. The death and Resurrection of Jesus brought into being the Christian Church as God's instrument for men and women to know, love and please God in this life and be happy with Him in the life to come. In this Church He offers responsibility to some men and women to care for their brothers and sisters in the way that good shepherds must look after their flocks, risking and even giving their lives if necessary. The history of the Church records many glorious examples of those who accepted this offer of responsibility and were faithful to God's trust in them, even to death. Names such as St Thomas a Becket, Janani Luwum, Oscar Romero and Martin Luther King come readily to mind.

On the other hand there have been in our own time, tele-evangelists who have been exposed as amassing great personal fortunes at the expense of God's people who trusted them as true ministers of the Gospel of Jesus Christ. Nor can we in the Anglican Church point too many fingers at others. There are clergy who make themselves fat, literally and figuratively, by feeding off the flocks entrusted to their care. As bishop I have had the painful experience of seeing a vicar in my Episcopal Area go to prison for misappropriating money given for the maintenance of the church's mission in the parish. Before she died, a successful author had set up a charitable trust and bequeathed the royalties of her books to this trust for the maintenance of the parish. As Vicar he became a trustee of this trust, so when he used these funds for his personal benefit he ran foul of Trustee law and was convicted and sent to prison. Here in Barbados, because of centuries of Establishment when the Anglican Church was fully financially supported by the State which paid clergy stipends, sextons' wages etc., maintained churches and graveyards, rectories and vicarages, congregations were not expected to give all that much to the Church. This was in stark contrast to the various denominations, many of which practised tithing, that is, giving one-tenth of their income to their church. As a result when the Anglican Church was disestablished Anglicans had no tradition of realistic giving, and no amount of fish-fries and so on could substitute for sacrificial giving. So today's clergy are under great pressure to be highly money-conscious. This exposes them to temptation to neglect routine, necessary parish work in order to earn extra money. Should this happen they would have become people who have accepted partnership with God with accountability to Him, but have betrayed His trust.

So it is of the greatest importance that congregations exercise a duty of care for their clergy. Clergy must be paid adequate stipends, adequate housing allowances, adequate travelling and office expenses and provided with some secretarial help. They must not assume anything, they must make sure that these things are in place.

Finally, there is a sense in which every single one of us is in a partnership with God which carries accountability to Him. But we need help from one another. First, we must pray for one another. 'More things are wrought by prayer than this world dreams of.' Secondly, we must offer financial help to those in need who may not be known personally to us, by giving money to the Church earmarked for those in need, such as through the care-box or the 'Vicar's Discretionary Fund'. Thirdly, actual physical assistance, however small to those we know need such assistance but may be reluctant to ask for it because they do not want to lose a relationship of equal friendship by becoming an inconvenience. It is not enough to say, 'if she wants help she only has to say.'

The patient, long-suffering landowner was eventually forced to take action against the obdurate tenants and replace them with others. As Our Lord reminded the Jews, God can raise up children of Abraham from stones if necessary. You and I are loved by God but we are not indispensable. Let us pray that we do not betray God's trust when He says of us: 'They will respect My Son.'

35
Work

St Lawrence Church, Barbados, 3 August 2008

Ephesians, chapter 4 verse 28
Let him that stole steal no more: but rather let him
labour, working with his hands the thing which is good,
that he may have to give to him that needeth.

Work is a good thing. Work is of God. The purpose of work is to glorify God, by meeting human need. Our Lord Jesus described the activity of God the Father as work, and His own ministry as work, in John, chapter 5 verse 17 when He said: *My Father has never yet ceased His work, and I am working too.* And again in John, chapter 9 verse 4 *I must do the work of Him Who sent Me.* The Bible describes the creation of the world as God's work when it says that after six days He rested from His labours.

From the very beginning it became clear that, under God, human survival and progress depended on human work. Men and women had to eat, so crops had to be grown and reaped; animals had to be reared or hunted for food; fish had to be harvested from river, lake and sea. If a man did not work, he did not eat! This was clearly God's plan for His world, and His gift of seasonal rain and sunshine ensured that human labour was rewarded with success. Indeed a man's work was so much a part of him, that in time men came to be identified by their work and their work became part of their names. So Joseph the carpenter became Joseph Carpenter, James the mason became James Mason, Robert the tailor became Robert Taylor and so on. Peter the farmer even became Peter Farmer! And St Paul, remembering that God calls on us to love others as much as we love ourselves, reminds us that the purpose of this labour is not only to meet our own need, but to give to others who are in need.

But work is not the same as employment. Employment is activity for which you are paid. All work is essential for human good, but not all employment serves the human good. For example, from the creation of humanity, the most important work in human endeavour could not be demeaned by being made into employment. There is no work known to humanity, and no work more important to the world, than that of a woman giving birth and caring for a child. On that work hangs the whole existence of the entire human race and that could never be thought of as employment. Employment can be measured in money, but a mother's sacrificial love cannot be measured or quantified.

On the other hand, there are forms of employment that are downright ungodly and sinful. I have long been haunted by a television interview I saw with a fresh-faced young American girl employed making guns and bombs in a munitions factory, and saying: 'I know war kills people, and I am sorry, but it is the only way I can do my job.' I think also of scientists, men gifted by God with the best intellectual powers, kissing their wives and children goodbye every morning, and going off to their laboratories trying to invent new ways of killing more and more people. Some years ago while here in Barbados on holiday, I read the remarks of a woman senator who was arguing for the legalising of prostitution on the grounds that it would provide employment for young women! I was scandalised to learn that she was a leading member of our Anglican Church, and phoned the Bishop to ask if her Rector or anyone else was in touch with her to find out how she reconciled her proposal with her Christian understanding of human worth and dignity and the teaching of the Christian Church.

Work is so much a part of God's order that if you are able-bodied and choose to live in idleness when there is real work to be done, you are defying God and living in sin. The amount of money you have has nothing to do with it. The politicians may glamourise idleness for their own purposes by reference to 'the boys on the block' but it is still sin. You are also stealing, because even to beg is to be stealing from someone who is unable to work and is in greater need than you are of the charity which is being given to you. There are many ways of stealing, such as borrowing with no intention of repaying, taking other people's property including when in employment the property entrusted to you by your employers, persistent late arrival for work and over-long lunch breaks, taking sick leave when there is nothing wrong with you, neglecting tasks in order to attend to personal affairs, withholding service until backhanders are offered, and denying service to those who offend you or are not members of your own political party or circle of acquaintance even though they are entitled to such service. These are all forms of stealing, and if you indulge in any of them, whoever you may be, you are a thief, and St Paul is speaking to you when he says: 'Let him that stole, steal no more.' In other words, stop it!

It is a sad fact, but a fact that has to be faced, that our nation was born in slavery. Slavery distorted human relations and created a number of unsatisfactory mental attitudes. These attitudes have remained even though slavery itself has been abolished. This has left a number of undesirable features in our national life and culture, and among these is a regrettable, if under-standable, attitude to work, employment and stealing. It did not matter how hard a slave worked, there was no reward for his labour and his conditions did not improve. So his greatest achievements day by day were the avoidance of work and the successful theft of food. Even after the abolition of slavery, employment was scarce and people were paid for only one day's work at a time. So early in his working life the apprentice was advised by the older hands: 'Always leave some work for tomorrow.' The only people who worked all the time were those who were too shortsighted to see when the boss wasn't looking! Sadly, these attitudes are all too obvious among us today.

The Christian Church in every place is called to infect the world with righteousness. This must mean that it cannot accept without question everything that is considered part of the national life and culture, as though religion is merely part of the leisure and entertainment industry. The Christian who finds himself or herself among acquaintances who will not work or colleagues at work who engage in these dishonest practices, must refuse to engage in them, and must be prepared if challenged to defend his or her refusal on the grounds that he or she believes that God is seeing it all, and would not approve of his or her participation. He or she must not be misled by the seeming appearance that in Barbados only poor people seem to go to prison. God who lacks nothing, continues to work; Christ, the Son of God, worked as a carpenter. If work is good enough for God why should it be beneath any of us to work? Our nation's life would be transformed for the better if only half the number of people in church on Sundays were to witness to Christ in this way. You will need strength for this witness, and through God's grace given to you in His Word and the Sacrament of the altar, you will receive whatever help is necessary.

When I was in primary school, I was given a poem to

recite. It was about a headteacher preparing the school for a visit from the Schools' Inspector. He told the children that the Inspector was sure to ask them what was the shape of the earth. So he showed them his snuff-box which was round, and told them to remember his snuff-box and that would remind them that the earth is round. Now the headteacher was in Church every Sunday in his Sunday-best clothes, which included his special Sunday-best snuff-box, which happened to be square. The Inspector duly arrived, and sure enough, he asked the class what was the earth's shape. A bright, observant little boy promptly answered 'Square, Sir, on Sundays, round on other days!' If we neglect necessary work and steal when employed Monday to Saturday, it will be a case of 'Christian, Lord, on Sundays, unchristian on other days!'

36
Dangers for the Church Within and Without

170th Anniversary of St Lawrence
St Lawrence Church, Barbados, 8 November 2009

St Luke, chapter 24 verse 48
... ye are witnesses of these things.

Hundreds of small boys, including myself, received all or part of our primary schooling in the Southborough Boys' School building at Clifton Hill, near Mount Wilton sugar factory in St Thomas. Hundreds of boys, including myself, received part or all of our secondary schooling in the Barbados Academy school building at the corner of Constitution and Halls Roads in Bridgetown. Hundreds of boys, including myself, received all or part of our secondary schooling in the Combermere School building in Roebuck Street.

Not one of those three buildings exists today. The site of Southborough Boys' is now a car park; the site of the Barbados Academy is now the Mencea Cox roundabout, and the Roebuck Street site of the former Combermere is now a Transport Board bus depot.

But the building is not the school. The school is the community of persons engaged in preparing pupils for life in the world. The school and its purpose will continue long after the building has disappeared, because of the beliefs which are the foundations of its schooling. Certainly in the case of Southborough Boys' School under the headship of the late Frank H. Barker, these foundations could be summarised in the following four short statements.

1. We did not make ourselves. God made us, and it is our duty to please Him;
2. The Bible tells us that God sent His Son Jesus Christ into the world to show us how to please Him;
3. Men killed Jesus, but God raised Him from the dead;
4. Jesus taught that in order to please God, we should all love our neighbours as ourselves and live by the Golden Rule, namely: *Do unto others as you would have them do unto you.* [Matthew chapter 7 verse 12]

On these foundations was built our preparation for life in this world.

For the past week we have been giving thanks to God for this House of Prayer, the St Lawrence Church building, now over 170 years old. We pray that for as long as this building is serving God's purpose it will continue to exist, for even longer than another 170 years. But should it cease to serve God's purpose, it should cease to exist. But this building is not St Lawrence Church. St Lawrence Church is the community of baptised persons being prepared for life in the world to come. Whether this building is here or not after we have all passed on to life beyond the grave, the Church must continue to prepare future generations to please God in this life and be happy with Him in the next.

For it is to this that we as a Church are called to be witnesses and we do so by witnessing to the four fundamental revealed truths, namely

1. Our Creator God, Who is a God of love, is to be worshipped
2. God became human in the Person of Jesus Christ, the Incarnation
3. God raised Christ Jesus from the dead, the Resurrection, and

4. We are to live lives of sacrificial love.

These revealed truths are at the heart of our Christian faith, and are not optional or negotiable beliefs for a true follower of Christ.

Now a church building is subject to two kinds of dangers: dangers from outside such as storms, hurricanes and so on, and dangers from inside, such as termites eating away foundations and pillars. The Church itself is also subject to these two kinds of dangers. One such outside danger is hostile governments, hostile religions, cynics and unbelievers. Another outside danger is that in some countries the Church becomes so embedded in the local culture that the prophetic voice of the Church is never heard, and the political methods of Robert Mugabe and the financial methods of Allen Stanford find echoes in the affairs of the Church.

But great as such dangers are, the termite-like danger from inside is far greater. Sometimes it is ignorance on the part of self-appointed church leaders who peddle a comfortable prosperity religion, which makes their followers feel good, and make themselves rich. But even within the ranks of the ordained ministers of the historic churches are to be found those whose ignorance, arrogance and lack of faith cause them to exhibit lack of belief in the Incarnation and the Resurrection, the two main pillars of the Christian faith.

Those accounts of Our Lord's earthly life authorised by the Church as the four canonical gospels of Matthew, Mark, Luke and John, make it clear that 'in the beginning was the Word and the Word was with God and the Word was God.' Jesus Himself told His disciples: 'I and the Father are one.' In his letter to the Philippians, chapter 2, St Paul says that Christ did not allow equality with God to prevent Him from becoming human.

It is on this revealed truth, and the authority of the Church, not the whim of the individual minister, that we as Christians believe in the unique dignity and worth of human personality. This human nature, elevated by God becoming human, is desecrated when persons are starved of food, clean water, medicines and the means of protecting and rearing their children, because some of us are so greedy that we grab for ourselves more than a fair share of the resources God has provided for all. It is desecrated when torture, violence and the use of guns and military power rob weaker persons of their God-given rights to life, liberty and the pursuit of happiness. Our objection to such desecration stems from our belief that God became incarnate in the Person of Jesus Christ. If we do not believe this we can find all sorts of justifications for our own self-serving and indifference while others suffer. Without the belief in the Incarnation can we uphold the sanctity of human life? And why should slavery be wrong? For anyone to undermine this fundamental doctrine is to do the work of termites in the Church.

This is no less true when we consider the Church's fundamental belief that God raised Christ Jesus from the dead in what we call the Resurrection. The earliest Christians were persecuted, hunted, burnt at the stake, murdered, fed to lions for the entertainment of rulers, all because they insisted that God had raised Christ from the dead. St Paul's preaching and teaching so strongly asserted Christ's Resurrection, that the Epicureans and Stoics in Athens thought that he was speaking about two gods, one named Jesus and the other named Resurrection. Acts, chapter 17 verse 18. In his letter to the Corinthians [1 Corinthians, chapter 15 verse 13] he points out that if Christ was not raised our faith is in vain. Why then do some modern church leaders find it so difficult to refer to the Resurrection, even at Easter? Is there the feeling that if Christ was not raised, then we ourselves will not be raised, so we will not have to give account for our share in the world's greed and corruption?

And if we do not believe that Jesus was raised from the dead, how can our prayers be other than lifeless, superficial and insincere, because to whom do we think we are speaking when we pray? Other people who themselves have a closer relationship with the living Lord Jesus will recognise that we are saying words into a vacuum, not conversing confidently to Someone with Whom we are well acquainted.

Those who love buildings and care for them know how important it is to inspect them regularly so that evidence of rot or termites can be treated. The People of God have a similar need. Occasions such as anniversaries are not for looking back only; or for self-congratulation on past achievements only. They are times for self-examination in the light of the known will of God, to ask God's forgiveness for past failures and to seek His help for the years ahead. In other words, they are occasions for self-examination, stocktaking, repentance and renewal. This does not make us any better or any worse than those who see no fault in themselves, only more open to God's Holy Spirit. It is by the help of this Holy Spirit, that whether or not this St Lawrence Church building goes on for another 170 years, or disappears from the face of the earth tomorrow. The witness to the Incarnation and the Resurrection by our worship of our Creator God in prayer and our lives of active sacrificial love must continue, so that men and women may be helped to prepare for the life in the world to come. We, the Church of Christ in St Lawrence, must not fail our Lord in this.

37
Christ the King

Festival of Christ the King
St Lawrence Church, Barbados, 22 November 2009

In those days there was no king in Israel; every man did what was right in his own eyes.

Today is the Church's festival of Christ the King, hence the Gospel for the day, which has just been read, is the account of the encounter between Pontius Pilate the Roman Governor in Jerusalem, and Jesus who had been brought before him by the Jewish Authorities for him to pronounce the death sentence on Him. The Jewish Authorities had decided that Jesus was a threat to their position and had convicted Him on the trumped-up charge of threatening to destroy the temple. But they wanted Him crucified and only the Roman Governor could pronounce that sentence. So they told the Roman Governor that Jesus was threatening revolt against the Romans because He was claiming to be the authentic King of the Jews. The inference was that if Pilate did not condemn Jesus to death and there was an uprising against the Roman occupiers, it would be Pilate's own fault.

Pilate really had no sympathy with these blackmailers and their vendetta against the pathetic figure before him, so he went through the motions of asking Jesus if He was King of the Jews, expecting Him to reply 'No, Your Honour.' He would then dismiss the case. He was surprised when Jesus replied that His kingdom was not of this world. There then ensued a dialogue between them, both using the same words, but meaning completely different things. Eventually Pilate put that famous question to Jesus: 'What is truth?' The irony is that as he asked that question he was literally staring Truth in the face, and not only Truth, but the Way, the Life, the Resurrection and the King of Kings. There are times when God says one thing to us, and we hear something completely different.

You may have noticed that although as is the custom I gave a verse from the Bible as the text for this sermon, *In those days there was no king in Israel, every man did what was right in his own eyes* I did not give a biblical reference. This is because the identical verse is found in two places in the Bible. It is found at Judges, chapter 17 verse 6, and Judges, chapter 21 verse 25. In both instances there is the suggestion that unrighteous actions were carried out because there was no king to enforce the laws, either in regard to the worship of false gods, or in the treatment of other tribes.

But scholars take widely differing views about the significance of this verse. Some argue that before there were kings in Israel, every man knew that it was his personal responsibility to obey the Ten Commandments. His conscience in the sight of God was what dictated his behaviour. God was Israel's only king, and He spoke to them through His prophets. So having a king like the other nations was a backward step, because the king's laws could only refer to their outward actions and not to their hearts and minds. There is a stark illustration of this contrast recorded in 1 Samuel, chapter 15. The prophet Samuel had given Saul, the first king of Israel, God's instruction that after victory in battle against the Amalekites no spoil was to be taken. When Samuel arrived he discovered that Saul had indeed kept sheep and cattle, thus disobeying God, but claiming that he had done it in order to offer them in sacrifice. This led Samuel to rebuke him in the words we know so well: 'to obey God is better than sacrifice.' In other words the inner submission of the heart and will to God is more important than the outward conformity to the King's wishes. So it was that when Jesus told Pilate that his kingdom was not of this world, he was referring to that total submission to God's will which we call the Kingdom of Heaven, while the kingdom to which Pilate and the Jewish Authorities were referring was the exercise of earthly power.

However much you and I may recoil from confrontation, disagreement with others, pain and suffering, there will always be time when as Christians our allegiance to Christ and our hopes for the kingdom of heaven will demand that we obey God's will and act according to our conscience even if this brings us into conflict with others, and even with the law itself.

As Bishop of Croydon at confirmation services I used to ask the newly confirmed to stand and face the congregation. I would then ask the congregation to give them loud and prolonged applause. Afterwards I would explain that this was a demonstration with a purpose because they would be asked to witness to their faith in today's world where it can be very lonely for a Christian, and where sometimes they may be the only person in their workplace to stand up for what is right, what is true, what is honest and just, in the name of the Lord Jesus. People will be saying to them 'how can it be wrong when we are all doing it' and 'why do you have to be different, who do you think you are?' So to keep the peace they will be tempted to go along with the crowd, and if they do so, then after that first giving-in, the second would become easier and eventually they would give up standing up for what is right. So I would say to them, 'when the devil speaks to you like that in your left ear, tempting you, I want you to hear in your right ear the sound of this applause which will remind you that when you stand up for Jesus you are not alone because not only those present in church today, but unseen millions of other Christians around the world are supporting you with their prayers'. So when you stand up for Jesus you are not alone. There are always more with you than those who are against you.

Today in Barbados it would be easy to forget that there is a difference between the kingdom of heaven and the kingdoms of this world. Here we do not suffer persecution for being Christian; on the contrary, church life is sometimes treated as an extension of the nation's leisure and entertainment industry. On the radio some time ago, I heard a commentator say, 'I really must congratulate Father X on an excellent sermon at a funeral yesterday. I have never in my whole life heard so many people laugh so much at a funeral.' People seem to expect preachers to entertain rather than edify or exhort them to a conscientious examination of their relationship with Christ, or call on them to face up to the hard and painful demands of the Gospel, and certainly not to regard themselves as sinners in need of God's mercy, not even in death. In our culture we find it difficult to say sorry, even to God. There are even reports of applause at the end of sermons, and preachers singing in the pulpit! Every big church occasion must now include the giving of awards as though we are doing Christ a favour by attending church in response to His own unconditional love for us. The truth is that if Jesus had been the kind of person depicted by this complacent, unchallenging version of religion, with which we seem so comfortable, no one would have bothered to crucify him!

But the more the official Churches find accommodation with the values of the kingdoms of this world, seeking security through wealth, material possessions and the patronage of those in power, the more necessary it becomes for us as individuals to be faithful to Christ's kingdom and to do what is right in His eyes even if it means standing alone. We may suffer ridicule, ostracism, hatred, and all forms of injustice. We may even be scorned as losers by our peers in career, occupation and profession, because as Bishop Lesslie Newbigin puts it in his book entitled *The Other Side of 1984*: 'There is now a public structure of truth which ignores God, and centres on the successful free-wheeling individual.' We may even have to witness unto death. It is significant that the earliest crucifixes showed Jesus on the cross, dressed as a king signifying that it is through suffering that Christ reigns. Like Pontius Pilate the world will not understand. It did not understand then, and does not understand now, when Christ says 'my kingdom is not of this world.'

38
40th Anniversary of the Cave Hill Campus

University of the West Indies
St Michael's Cathedral, Barbados, 12 October 2003

Let us pray: Come among us Holy Spirit, and open our ears that we may hear; open our minds that we may know; open our hearts that we may love, so that hearing, knowing and loving, we may follow where you lead in spirit and in truth. Amen.

St John, chapter 8 verse 32 Jesus said:
You will know the truth,
and the truth will set you free.

In many churches around the world, Christians regularly pray from universities and other places of learning. We pray that they may be enlightened by God's Spirit so that the whole world may be filled with the knowledge of His Truth. Truth is the apprehension of things as they *are*, rather than as we would like them to be, and because this world is God's creation, truth is like a law of gravity, always pulling us toward God. The genuine pursuit of truth takes us in the direction of God, so the acquisition and dissemination of knowledge, the very purpose of a university's existence, makes it God's instrument.

Truth is so important that those who would displace God or wield supreme power over His creation, claim for themselves the right to make truth. In the unlamented Soviet system, for example, truth was what the State said it was. In our day, the calculated manipulation of truth via the mass media (euphemistically called 'spin doctoring') can effectively empty democracy of its substance. I remember also, during the Watergate crisis in Washington, President Nixon's spokesman saying to reporters at a Press Conference: 'All that I said to you yesterday is now inoperative.' 'Are you saying that yesterday you told us a pack of lies?' asked a reporter. 'I am saying,' replied the spokesman, 'that it is now inoperative.' So, not unlike the Church itself, the university can never be entirely embedded in any political system, or national culture, neither can it bend the knee to any vested interest no matter how powerful or how generous, because it must always have a prior loyalty to God's truth.

That is not to say that the university should stay aloof from the community in which it is set. Quite the contrary. The 'ivory-tower' concept of academia is no more tenable in today's world than is stratification of society based on birth. What is more, we have it on no less authority than Christ Himself, that truth (to which the university is committed) has a particular and important fruit. In John's Gospel, chapter 8 verse 32, Jesus says: *You will know the truth, and the* truth *will set you* free. The fruit of truth is freedom, and freedom of body, mind and spirit is God's will for all his children.

The fruit of truth is freedom. This strikes an immediate and special chord with us here in the Caribbean. Like all human beings born into this world, we were born in sin, and our freedom from the destructive power of sin is effected by the sacrificial death of Christ, and his grace which gives birth to our faith in Him. We who are alive in the Caribbean today, share with our forebears this spiritual freedom as sons and daughters of God.

But the freedom that we have which they did not have, is freedom of the *body*. For more than 200 years their bodies were literally owned by other people. Freedom of their bodies only came with the abolition of slavery, and slowly, slowly, over the years, step by step, has come also the political freedom we now enjoy.

But what of freedom of the *mind*? Political freedom can be won by armed struggle as in Haiti, by revolution as in Cuba, or it can be conceded as in other parts of the Caribbean. But freedom of the body from slavery and colonial occupation is no guarantee of freedom of the mind. Only a few weeks ago I overheard a woman proclaiming loudly: 'You don't buy what you can beg for!' And a very popular calypso in this year's cropover activities declared: 'Don't talk to muh if yuh ain't gi'ing me nothing'. The bodies of free persons with the minds of slaves. Very little pride here and even less industry!

Long before the term 'brainwashing' came into popular usage a tapestry of selective instruction, conformity, imitation and so-called traditions and conventions, ensured that vision was restricted, ambition thwarted, and success awarded to those who protected the status quo, rather than won by those whose freedom of mind and spirit led them to question it. In other words, forces conspired to keep our minds enslaved. They have been more successful than ever they could have hoped for!

It is said that when Mr Nehru, Prime Minister of India, was asked what he thought of European civilisation, he replied: 'It would be a very good idea.' In the Caribbean today, at every level of society and not least among our political and professional classes, freedom of the mind would be a very good idea.

True freedom is the fruit of truth, so synthetic truth produces synthetic freedom. If we are to be truly free, we must look truth in the face however unpalatable that might be, and our university must help us to do so.

For that reason, we challenge and call upon the most able minds in the Caribbean, including those in this university to think deeply upon the mystery of Jesus the Word-made-flesh, and his words when He says: '*I am the Truth*'. Do not be intellectually lazy and dismiss Christianity because in our society it is so often overlaid with 'Churchianity' and opportunism. Or say that all religions are the same. Through the eyes of Jesus we can see some of what our freedom is to be *from*, and what it is *for*.

One of the early symbols of Christ, especially in Christian art, was the fish. Jesus used the fish to teach that we mush accept no substitute for the real thing. In Matthew, chapter 7 verse 10 He said that a father should not give his son a serpent when he asked for a fish. Today we can use the word itself – F-I-S-H – to remind us of what we are to be freed *from* and what we are to be freed *for*.

First, we must have freedom from fear of *victimisation* so that we can have the freedom to be frank, open and honest in our dealings with one another. For we can be so crippled by fear of victimisation that we can become bad neighbours and irresponsible citizens. We witness blatant criminal activity but refuse to inform or co-operate with the police. Fear of victimisation makes us collude with exploitation and abuse of ourselves and others by those set in authority over us. It makes us remain silent about work practices which defraud employers, and it makes ours a culture of much grumbling and the long 'choops' but never a reasonable, careful complaint, therefore no accountability and no improvement – 100 per cent Bajan!

But being frank with one another means speaking the truth in love while recognising our own shortcomings.

Secondly, we must be free from *insularity* and the arrogance that goes with it. In today's world, insularity is a state of mind. We cannot but be affected by events in Iraq, Afghanistan, Liberia etc., but we can still behave as though these places are not only foreign – but on a different planet altogether – and far less important than a dubious umpiring decision against Brian Lara! We can continue to believe that the way we have always done things is the way everyone should do them, and the way they should always be done.

One of the founding-fathers of Central Cricket Club at Vaucluse, the team for which I played in the 1950's, was L.O. Wood, who as a young cricketer bowled for Barbados. Now in the evening of his days, he was invited to play again for the club in a Celebrities Festival Match at Vaucluse, and he opened the bowling to Roy Marshall the attacking Barbados and West Indian opening batsman. Roy Marshall square cut his first delivery for four, cover drove the second for four, and drove the third back past the bowler for four. This was too much for the Grand Old Man. He stood on the pitch, arms akimbo, glared at Marshall and declared with withering scorn: 'And you call yourself an opening batsman – flashing at the new ball!'

Incidentally, some years ago I wrote to Roy Marshall to let him know that I planned to use this incident in a sermon. He wrote back to say that on that occasion the Old Man had also said something more, but he didn't think a bishop could repeat it in church!

So it is true that we may have ways of doing things which have served us well in the past and have been the envy of others. But the world has not been standing still and changing conditions require changed approaches. The University must help our Caribbean nations to identify those habits, customs and conventions that have outlived their usefulness, and point us in the direction of new ideas and initiatives.

In this connection I was interested to read in the press recently, a report that the University and the West Indies Cricket Board are searching for a title in relation to the common concept of nationhood. Could it be that at long last the European mis-naming of the Caribbean, with its divisive colonial overtones of British West Indies, Dutch West Indies, French West Indies will be corrected and the 'West Indies Cricket Board' replaced by the 'Caribbean Nations Cricket Board', and that at some time in the future we will be able to rejoice in the more self-descriptive titles of 'The University of the Caribbean at Barbados', 'The University of the Caribbean at Jamaica', 'The University of the Caribbean at Trinidad', in place of the Cave Hill, Mona, and St Augustine campuses of the University of the West Indies? Has not the term 'West Indies' outlived its usefulness? Nationhood has come to the Caribbean and the University has an important role in helping with the transformation of our people from colonial *subjects*, who are given *favours*, to self-determining *citizens* who must bear the heavy responsibilities of people who have *rights*. This demanding role will be further strengthened when able students from Martinique and Guadeloupe, Aruba, Bonaire and Curacao make this campus their first choice of university.

Thirdly, we are to be free for *sharing* and *sacrifice* and freed from *selfishness* and *self-importance*. We do well to remember that every person is someone created in God's image, and someone for whom Christ died. That is the person's true worth – worth that can neither be enhanced nor diminished by birth, ethnic origin, gender, nationality or even academic achievement! We brought nothing into this world, and it is certain that we can carry nothing out. Once when a very wealthy man died, someone asked: How much money did he leave? And received the reply: '*All* of it.' So the big fish in our Caribbean ponds may need to be reminded that these ponds are really very small, in that in the face of a God whose majesty and mercy are beyond our comprehension, human self-importance is both unbecoming and pitiable. How thrilled I was one Friday evening to be served at a fried fish stall in Oistin by a graduate of an English university who was lending her mother, the stall holder, a helping hand.

We must be free for *sharing*. Sharing is not the same as giving and it is not the same as receiving. It is both – a mutual exchange among equals in community. It is at the heart of Christian living, initiated by Christ Himself when at the Last Supper He shared Bread and wine with those He did not call 'servants' or 'followers' but 'friends'. St Paul urged Jews and Gentiles to share their spiritual and material gifts. Sharing must be the hallmark of our Caribbean life. In that spirit, we who have received so much from others must not begrudge the world community the services of our brightest sons and daughters. When they leave us to serve in international agencies and institutions, they must not be derided as 'deserters', but recognised as front-line troopers, and supported in every way. In a world where the self-interest of large and powerful nations may cloud the vision of their representatives in the various international endeavours, persons whose own countries have no military muscle or financial power with which to threaten others, may be more acceptable as impartial go-betweens and peacemakers. This may be the role for Caribbean personnel. God will provide such persons. It is for the Caribbean to nurture them, and the University to equip them.

With this in mind, graduates from our Caribbean universities must not limit their sights to the Caribbean or to a particular territory in the region. Nor must they tailor their development to meet perceived short-term needs if such tailoring means curtailing their personal growth. They do not know what God has in store for them. There is much wisdom in T.S. Eliot's advice: 'Take no thought for the reaping – only for proper planting'.

Fourthly, we must free ourselves from *hypercriticism of others* and instead be free to *honour* them. There is a rightful place for *constructive* criticism, because criticism is necessary for self-examination and improvement. But there is also a destructive kind of criticism, devoid of any praise, encouragement or helpful advice, which drains other people of self-esteem. We should bear in mind that there are some people with a high degree of self-knowledge who are only too aware of the faults they have which irritate and alienate others. They have a perpetual struggle with these faults and need every encouragement not to give up that struggle. An insensitive or scathing condemnation of the 'Thank-God-I-am-not-like-you' variety, could be the last straw to drive them to despair.

We must be free to honour everyone. This may mean watching someone excel in a sphere which is beyond us and saying to ourselves: 'That is not a gift God has given me, but I rejoice that He has given it to her.' In Ephesians, chapter 5 verse 21, we are instructed: *Be subject to one another for the sake of Christ.* The writer saw a community of people with differing gifts, but with circular accountability in which the highest-placed and the lowest-placed persons are equally accountable to one another, honouring and respecting each other. Would it were like this in Barbados and the rest of the Caribbean! How wonderful it would be if we could be assured of the same painstaking, courteous, cheerful service from every sales assistant, every civil servant, every policeman whether we are easily recognisable celebrities on the one hand, or elderly, poorly-dressed rustics on the other. But we in Barbados know only too well, that it is not *who* you know – it is whom!

F-I-S-H. Freedom from fear of victimisation, from insularity, from self-importance and from hyper-criticism of others, and freedom for frank speaking, for ideas and initiatives for service and for honouring others.

We are here today to give God thanks for forty years of the Cave Hill Campus. It will be some time before we are able to give the same answer as that given to the American tourist who was admiring the perfectly groomed lawns of the Oxford University colleges and asked what was the secret. 'Well, you water the lawns and cut the grass, and you water the lawns and cut the grass, and you do that for 700 years, and this is what you have.' Compared with that, forty years may not appear a long time, but in the Caribbean much has happened in this period and this campus has played its part. Its history makes impressive reading. Reading an account of its beginnings I found vicarious pleasure in the camaraderie enjoyed by the very first undergraduates even when the voice of their lecturer was drowned out by the rain bearing down on the galvanised roofs of their makeshift lecture-room huts! I envied the freedom enjoyed by the early administrators who had to find their own solutions to new problems without the hindrance of red tape! And how satisfying it must be in these later years for those who worked behind the scenes in those early days, to know that their efforts have borne such magnificent fruit. They were in at the beginning of a forty-year-long essay in co-operation. In physical space and buildings, in breadth of services, in increase of personnel, and in profile and influence in the community, this Cave Hill Campus has grown almost beyond recognition. For this we thank

God, and we echo sentiments usually sung lustily at other times and in other places:

Wider still and wider, shall thy bounds be set
God who made thee mighty, make thee mightier yet.

Yet if it is to look truth in the face, and retain a name synonymous with freedom of thought, speech and action, this campus will also be a home for unpopular causes. And in that regard I would still like to see a place found in the Caribbean, whose scholarship was acknowledged by the academic world more than 300 years ago, and who can be described as the first great pioneer of university education for Caribbean people. I refer of course to Sir Christopher Codrington, whose college here in Barbados helped to mould the minds of many, who in their turn, played some part in shaping what we have today. It is not without significance that he considered spiritual health and physical health equally necessary for the well-being of the person.

Thanks to the existence of this Cave Hill Campus these past forty years, there are now thousands of families in Anguilla, Antigua, Barbados, Barbuda, Dominica, Grenada, Montserrat, Nevis, St Kitts, St Lucia, St Vincent and other territories, who now boast their first university graduate member. This does not mean that these young persons are the first bright or even the most able members of their families. Rather they come from a long line of hardy men and women, the labours of whose hands, hands gnarled by the canecutter's cutlass or domestic 'jooking-board', and backs bent double by heavy bundles of bananas and sugar cane, still had to be augmented by quick and nimble minds and practical good sense in order for them to survive and make ends meet. These parents, grandparents and great-grandparents had the same natural talent and potential as these later generations but no clouds were provided for *them* to float on! But it is this campus that has made possible this first and following generations of university graduates, and it owes it to them to warn that it is not enough to be committed to excellence. *How* they excel and what they do with their excel-lence are equally important. In other words, there is and should be a moral and spiritual dimension to academic success.

You graduates and undergraduates must excel *fairly*. Being first to the line has no merit if instead of outrunning the others you merely impeded them. And if after your academic success you become mere spectators of other people's struggles, watching them flounder in the water with no thought of helping them, this campus has failed you. You must *care*. Do not lose your humanity in pursuit of *any* goal, however desirable. Your God is a God of love, and justice is the communal expression of love. You must do for others what others have done for you. Excellence, fairness and concern must be your personal way of saying thanks to God and thanks to your ancestors.

But to do this in today's world where self-interest and the acquisitive instinct are rampant will require a considerable amount of inner freedom, and for this you must give serious thought to the claims of Jesus Christ. For whatever sacrifices God may call on you to make, they will not include the sacrifice of your intellect. Without despising the simple faith of others you must devote the best powers of your mind and spirit to understanding God's way with the world, and His will for you. Although you need to look no further than Jesus Christ, such is the depth of His unfathomable riches, that in this quest every sinew of your being can be engaged and stretched. He was tempted to put God to the test – as you will be; He was tempted to use the gifts God had given Him to meet His own material needs – as you will be; He was tempted to give his allegiance to Evil as a short cut to power – as you will be. Other people will attempt to use and abuse you, flatter, mock and deride you, accept good at your hands but desert you in your hour of need; close friends may even betray you. All this was done to Jesus, and some of it may be done to you. It is a far cry from the glib promises of material prosperity in this life, and heaven in the next which you may get from those preaching a cosy, respectable undemanding religion of a Jesus meek and mild, holding hands with little children. But Christianity is a grown-up religion for grown-up people in a tough and grown-up world, and Evil has many faces, not all of them snarling and unattractive. To be sure you will have times of doubt – who doesn't – Jesus himself did, but this does not mean lack of faith. Like Jesus carrying the cross you will fall – perhaps more than once. What will give you the necessary inner freedom is the knowledge that you did not make yourself; that it is no accident that you are who you are and where you are; that God's purpose for you is rooted in the sacrificial love of Jesus, and that you are a twosome with Him whose strength partners your weakness. The knowledge of this truth will make you free, and you will walk even through the valley of the shadow of death, and fear no evil.

39

'To educate or to train –
that is the question.'

The Summer Meeting of the Society of
Headmasters and Headmistresses of Independent Schools
Royal Russell School, Croydon, Surrey, UK 9 June 1994

Mr Chairman, Ladies and Gentlemen. Thank you very much for your invitation to address you and for your generosity in allowing me to choose the theme of my address. I am reminded of the story of the divinity student preparing for an Old Testament examination. He had studied the sequence of questions in the past exams and was confident that there would be a question on the kings of Israel and Judah. Alas, when the time came there was no such question. Instead he was asked to 'compare and contrast the prophets Elijah and Elisha.' So he began his answer: 'Far be it from me to compare and contrast two such great men. Rather, let us consider, the kings of Israel and Judah.'

I begin with this story because last autumn I was invited to address the Headmasters Conference at their annual meeting and used the occasion to urge them to stand firm against the forces that would convert them from being 'educators' into 'trainers.' I argued then that our Christian faith is a world faith with a particular morality.

As Christians our understanding of morality is of the God revealed to Humankind in Jesus Christ. The essential character of this God is *love*, and every single person is someone created in His image, and someone for whom Christ died. This is the person's true worth, and this worth can neither be enhanced nor diminished by circumstances of birth, ethnic origin, gender, colour, disability or even achievement. Our moral standard is the mind of Christ, and this is how we know that God's love for us should be reflected in our love for one another. All use of power, authority and decision-making should be directed to this end.

By World Faith it is not meant that Christianity should dominate the world to the exclusion of every other creed to which women and men may give allegiance. Rather that it is *universal* – open to every human being, irrespective of nationality, gender, ethnic group, colour or language, who encounters Jesus, and also that there is no individual or nation to whom Christian truth is not applicable. The essence of this truth is that human beings are to love God totally and to love fellow human beings no more and no less than they love themselves. The lesson of the life, death and Resurrection of Jesus is that so binding is this truth, that if in our pursuit of it death comes to us, as it did to Him, so be it.

But here in Britain we are fast becoming a society in which financial gain is the overriding measure of every human activity. The *theory* might be to create a high-tech society of high pay and high living standards and to 'squeeze inflation out of the system'; the product is an ever-expanding underclass of people who, in Professor Ralf Darendorf's chilling phrase, are literally 'not needed.' People become expendable, and whether they are geriatrics in old people's homes, convicts in prisons, or those who are incapable of looking after themselves, to care for them is now seen as a burden, and a millstone around the necks of the rest of us. Beware the siren voices of those urging the desirability of euthanasia!

How else can we explain our Government's invitation to us to buy shares in prisons and make a profit from the incarceration of fellow citizens, running the risks of decision making policemen, magistrates and judges developing a personal interest in keeping jails full, and of crime syndicates obtaining substantial interests in companies owning or running prisons? How else can we explain the spectre of black women in 1793 dying while being *im*ported into this country in chains, and in 1993 a black woman dying while being *de*ported from this country in chains? But such things will be if there is no morality in the ordering of our affairs. This very day the elections for the European Parliament are being held, and I was disappointed although not surprised that one of the major political parties has played the race card by suggesting that should people vote for their opponents there would be increased 'immigration' – and we all know what that code-word means. This in spite of the increase in the number of racist assaults and murders in this country and the growing strength of neo-Fascism and neo-Nazism in Europe generally.

Years ago, while still at secondary school in Barbados, I came across the following words penned by my English master, Gordon Bell, in the introduction to a little book he had written:

The artist works on canvas, the sculptor with marble, the potter in clay, all of which must some day fall to pieces. So, too, must be the fate of the worker in wood and the worker in metal. But the teacher – his material is the living being fashioned in the image of his Maker. To help fill a mind with knowledge, and a heart with understanding … that is to share creation with God.

I believe Gordon Bell is right, and therefore as teachers, yours is an awesome responsibility.

You are *educators*, and must remain educators – resisting whatever pressures there may be to convert you into mere 'trainers', functionaries whose contribution is to fashion more and more cogs for the corporate machine. You may well be caught between the hammer of an officialdom whose life force is competitive capitalism, and the anvil of ambitious parents concerned primarily with success in whatever kind of society is on offer, and only secondarily with nature of that society. Yet as independent educators yours is the responsibility of educating the *spirit*. This means that you are to 'draw out' and fan that flame ignited by the divine spark which is in each of us. In the Epistle to the Philippians, chapter 4 verse 8, St Paul describes your task in these words, *And now, my friends, all that is true, all that is noble, all that is just and pure, all that is lovable and attractive, whatever is excellent and admirable, fill your thoughts with these things.*

A checklist like this – truth, nobility, justice, integrity, love, excellence, winsomeness – will soon have your students asking awkward questions. Why, for example, with the technological achievements of our age, half the people in the world still go to bed hungry each night, and 40,000 die each day of malnutrition-related diseases, the equivalent of a jumbo jet crashing and killing everyone on board every fifteen minutes of every day? Why are under-nourished Africans at war shooting at each other, not with bows and arrows but with the latest military hardware manufactured in *our* factories? Why across Europe and in this country are racist murders on the increase? Why are there so many miscarriages of justice coming to light and so many people convinced that there are many more? And in Oscar Wilde's trenchant words, are we still teaching our children the criminal calendar of Europe and calling it 'history'?

This is God's world, and He still calls us both as groups and individuals to share His love and concern, not only for us ourselves but for others. Obedience to His call, and a sense of responsibility commit us to the struggle for a social order, internationally and nationally, that is just, participatory and sustainable.

Now far be it from me to compare and contrast the Headmaster's Conference and the Society of Head-masters and Headmistresses of Independent Schools, but until two days ago I intended to expand on this theme in my address this morning. Then came to hand this publication from the Institute of Race Relations: *Outcast England – how schools exclude Black children.* It draws on statistics from surveys conducted by the Office for Standards in Education, the National Union of Teachers and the Commission for Racial Equality and shows black children are almost four times more likely to be suspended than white, and in Birmingham for example where black children were ten per cent of the school population, they were 40.3 per cent excluded children. Let me quote from the challenging intro-duction to the book: 'Exclusion is seldom the measure of a child's capacity to learn: it is an indication instead, of the teacher's refusal to be challenged. And when you have an education system which puts a premium, not on the educability of the child, but on the price of its education, the challenge to the teacher is the *financial* cost of keeping it in school, not the *human* cost of keeping it out. When, in addition educability itself is prejudiced in terms of societal stereotype which associates "black" with "problem", the exclusion of the black child becomes that much more automatic. Conversely, it is precisely because black children are already excluded, more than others, from most aspects of social life, that they need to be included, more than others, in the educational life of the school.'

The Royal Philanthropic Society Rectory Lodge opened by H.R.H. Duke of Edinburgh on 6 November 1992
shown here from left to right:
John Easton, Chairperson; H.R.H. Duke of Edinburgh, Patron; Wilfred Wood, President; Don Coleman, Director

Photo Basil Barnes

40
200th Anniversary of the Royal Philanthropic Society

Service of Thanksgiving
Southwark Cathedral, UK, 16 September 1998

1 John, chapter 4 verses 20-21
If a man say, I love God, and hateth his brother, he is a
liar: for he that loveth not his brother whom he hath
seen, how can he love God whom he hath not seen?
And this commandment have we from him,
That he who loveth God love his brother also.

The *occasion* of this act of worship today is the 200th
anniversary of the Royal Philanthropic Society. The
purpose of our worship is to thank God for whatever
good the Society has been able to achieve in the 200
years of its existence, and to ask His blessing and
guidance for its work in the years ahead. We are bold
enough to do this, because we are confident that the
aims of the Society are in accordance with the
purposes of God.

How do we know this?

All that we, as human beings, know of God, we know
through Jesus Christ, because we believe that in Jesus,
we see God in human form. In His life, His actions and
His teaching, Jesus showed that God is *love*. He
demonstrated that God's love is *active* bringing
forgiveness for offences against God and our fellows
which we call sin; freedom to those whose minds and
bodies are imprisoned, and healing and health to those
who are sick. And it is significant that when Christ
chose to indicate which human actions are of infinite

and eternal worth, and meritorious in God's sight, this is what He said, as recorded in St Matthew's Gospel, chapter 25 verses 31–41.

When the Son of Man comes in His glory and all the angels with Him, He will sit in state on His throne, with all the nations gathered before Him. He will separate men into two groups, as a shepherd separates the sheep from the goats, and He will place the sheep on His right hand and the goats on His left. Then the King will say to those on His right hand: 'You have My Father's blessing; come, enter and possess the Kingdom that has been ready for you since the world was made. For when I was hungry you gave Me food; when thirsty, you gave Me drink; when I was a stranger you took Me into your home; when naked you clothed Me; when I was ill you came to My help; when in prison you visited Me.' Then the righteous will reply: 'Lord, when was it that we saw You hungry and fed You, or thirsty and gave You drink, a stranger and took You home, or naked and clothed You? When did we see You ill or in prison and come to visit You?' And the King will answer: 'I tell you this, anything you did for one of my brothers here, however humble, you did for Me.'

So we may be sure that the Society's care for young people who are in the vulnerable period of transition from adolescence to adulthood, in danger of damaged self-esteem or at risk in other ways, is a work of which God approves. We thank Him for the opportunity to share in this work.

But what of the future? The founders of our Society 200 years ago were people of immense vision. Their philanthropic concern was not limited to people of their own social class, but rather represented their efforts to share their good fortune with other human beings whose great needs had come to their attention. Their pioneering, innovative searchlight of care, continues to be the hallmark of the Society's work today, as evidenced by the two triple-key projects, the Leaving Care Project and the Bail Support Scheme. But in 200 years the world has become a much smaller place, and the needs of God's children at the international, national and local levels are more clearly before our eyes than even the most far-seeing of our founders could have imagined. Some months ago I listened to a report on a conference of those agencies working to help people in the Developing World, and heard that every minute of every day, twenty people, eighteen of them children, die of starvation, malnutrition or other related diseases. A few days after hearing that report, I heard one of our MPs state, in a speech in the House of Commons, that each week the European Market spends more than one hundred million pounds on storing, dumping or destroying surplus foodstuffs!

In such bleak conditions in the developing world, where the struggle for survival occupies every waking moment, it would be inconceivable that thousands of young people are not at even greater risks than those known to us in this country. They too, must be our concern, because they are also God's children and or fellow men. So could it be that the questing, pioneering spirit of our Philanthropic Society points now to an overseas project, not only as a sign of the universality of God's concern, but also as a colour? In addition, our divided world today badly needs every action which gives people of one country reason to think with good will about people of another. We love God: we must also love our brothers and sisters in the way God wants us to do.

Today we pray in thanksgiving for the past and in

supplication for the future – that God's purpose may be worked out in the life of the Royal Philanthropic Society, and all of us, committee, workers and clients, may be found faithful in our several vocations.

41
The Shepherd's Bush Housing Association
Address to the Annual General Meeting
23 September 1991

Thank you for inviting me to speak to your Annual General meeting this evening. I was one of the founding members of the Association, and still remain an interested member so I am aware of the Association's role and importance within the local community. Its 2,300 homes have provided help to homeless people, elderly people and those with special housing needs in the borough.

Growth and consolidation must be kept in double-harness, and after many years of growth, the recent past has been a period of consolidation for this Association. In particular, the problem of disrepair in many of the Association's existing homes is being tackled. More than 400 properties were in need of repair at the beginning of 1991: half of these need at least £20,000 spent on them, and many need more than £100,000.

You will see that the Housing Corporation has been impressed by the programme you have put together to deal with the repair backlog, because over £3.5 million has been allocated in 1991/92 to help repair almost 100 individual homes. The regional office has already made a commitment to a further £0.5 million on 1992/3, and hopes to make more available once bids for the New Year have been assessed.

Overall, the Association has received £10 million from the regional office this year, reflecting The

Above: *Bishop Wilfred Wood Close, Peckham, South East London, entrance to housing development of the African Refugee Housing Action Group (ARHAG)*

Below: *The opening of Bishop Wilfred Wood Court, Pragel Street, Plaistow, East London, 27 May 1992,* shown here from left to right: *Lee Samuel, Founder Chairperson of Carib Housing Association; Wilfred Wood, and Lady Ina Wood*

Housing Corporation's support for action to repair properties, and to clear your pipeline of properties needing building works.

As you know, the Shepherd's Bush Housing Association is one of the key participants in the *Hounslow Partnership*. This initiative brings together eight housing associations on five consortium sites. Shepherd's Bush Housing Association will lead a small consortium on the Beverly Road School site in Chiswick. This will yield thirty new homes for homeless families using £1.8 million from the Housing Corporation. The scheme overall will produce 300 homes over two years for homeless people of Hounslow.

A success of the partnership was the willingness of the local authority, local housing associations, and the Housing Corporation's regional office to bring their resources and skills together. Although we must not be too self-congratulatory because so much remains to be done, we acknowledge the Association's important role in this process.

I understand that discussions are in their early stages about sites in Hammersmith and Fulham and I would expect that this Association will again wish to be involved.

I commend your work on *special needs schemes*, in which you have a note-worthy record, and also the success of Shepherd's Bush Housing Association's sales programme to first-time buyers.

Another particularly encouraging development is your co-operation with the Westway Housing Association. Westway Housing Association was registered with the Housing Corporation under the five year plan for Black Associations and this Association has offered valuable help and advice to Westway in its early years. I hope that this help can now be extended to transferring stock to them.

As the figures I have quoted show, a substantial amount of money is being channelled to housing associations through the Housing Corporation. Nationally, the figures are: £1.5 billion this year; £2 billion next year. And these figures will be boosted by what can be raised on the private market.

The Housing Corporation's job is to help turn that government money as quickly as possible into quality homes for people in need. The decision to give housing associations prime responsibility for the provision of new housing has greatly widened our responsibilities. As an organisation which is the prime recipient of government subsidy, the Corporation – like housing associations themselves – will properly be judged more stringently than before. Our claim to the level of funding we now receive, and any future claims to the level of funding we now receive, and any future claims will be judged by our ability to contribute to the solution of the country's most serious housing problems.

Such problems include:-

1) *Homelessness* – here the need is to provide new homes in areas of particular shortage; to make the best use of these and re-let homes to homeless people.

2) *Problem Local Authority Estates* – where poor repair, outdated facilities, and resident disaffection lead to under-use as well as abuse.

3) *Poor Housing Services* – where the need is to improve the quality of service to tenants offered by both the Local Authorities and the Housing Associations.

4) *Bridging the Gap between Incomes and House Prices* – to help those who wish to have a stake in the equity of their home.

The Corporation can help associations tackle these

problems. For example, the regulatory framework for associations is to be strengthened. We want to use our staff to improve the quality and extent of the Housing Corporation's supportive supervisory function. To this end we need more information from associations on the way they manage their organisations. For example, the Corporation's monitoring officers are coming to you here at Shepherd's Bush next month to assess performance, and the monitors will look at the Management Committee's controls of the Association through target-setting, and the receipt of reports from its officers on the meeting of such targets, and so on.

It is important that we improve our information on associations' performances so that we can satisfy ourselves and demonstrate to Government, to other authorities and to you that public investment in Association stock is reaching those for whom it is intended, namely those in need.

There are other considerations we believe to be important:-
1) What do the tenants themselves think of their association's performance?
2) What is the physical condition of the stock?

So, the Housing Corporation will:-
1) be requiring housing associations to demonstrate tenant satisfaction by regular surveys of tenant opinion, and you should know that this will have a bearing on the level of new allocations. Allocations will go exclusively to housing associations that are good housing *managers*, and to developers, however good they may be, only insofar as they are also good managers, and
2) work with housing associations on a better assessment of stock condition, which should lead to more accurate prediction of medium/long term repairs.

I can appreciate that with the recent departure of Peter Norman your Chief Executive, the Association is in a *crucial* phase of its existence. But every crucial moment does not have to become a crisis. I read somewhere once that 'crucial moments first become crises when oxen and hotheads get excited'. You have been very fortunate in securing the part-time services of Caroline Pickering, a veteran trouble-shooter, not unaccustomed to picking her way through minefields, but there is a limit to what even miracle-workers can do! You will not be surprised that I cannot resist the temptation to quote the Bible, and I remember Judges, chapter 21 verse 25 *In those days, there was no king in Israel – every man did what was right in his own eyes.* I sincerely hope this is not true in this Association, because there are a number of things that need to be done, and the role of the Management Committee is central and crucial.

1) You must plan for the future and set targets;
2) You must ensure, by staff reports etc that these targets are being met;
3) You must give consideration to your rate of future growth and your structure for handling this;
4) You will bear in mind that you are part of a *Movement*, and a Movement is powered by the *spirit* of that Movement. That spirit is a determination to provide homes for people in greatest need, and homes that protect and reflect their human dignity as sons and daughters of a God who is *their* Father and *our* Father.

I am in a position to say all of this because I was in on the birth of this Association. In the mid 1960s John Asbridge was Vicar and I was Honorary Curate at St Stephen's Shepherd's Bush. We found that a number of our parishioners, many of them African and West Indian, living in large over-crowded terraced houses, were being displaced every time these houses were bought for conversion by housing associations. As we could not win a deal with these housing associations to re-house our parishioners we decided to form our own housing association. So, with Revd John Asbridge as chairman, my wife as secretary/typist, the two churchwardens and some other folk we have recruited as committee members [all voluntary, of course] and with the aid of the church's duplicating machine, the Shepherd's Bush Housing Association was born. I can well remember the exhilaration we felt as we swept up after the builders, and laid the lino ourselves in our first house in Hammersmith Grove and moved our first tenants in. I moved to Catford in 1974 and soon after that I resigned from the Committee because I found I could no longer have the personal contact with the tenants [we did our own house to house rent collecting in those days] and employees of the Association that I felt was necessary for a committee member if he/she is not to be become an absentee landlord. Present committee members, take note!

I could say a lot more, but I must not bore you. I prize meaningful tenants' participations in the affairs of housing associations and I congratulate you on your progress in this. I advocate the retention of a strong volunteer element in the work of associations, and I urge responsible exercise of power by a Management Committee whose members find time to keep abreast of what is required of them. So I congratulate you and wish you all well in this worthwhile endeavour, but remind you of what they say about people who live in glass houses – they have to answer the door bell!

Notes on the text

2. Life Experience With Britain

This talk was part of a series chaired in 1999 by the late John La Rose, writer, publisher, activist, civil rights and social justice champion and chairman of the George Padmore Institute. The series was the second of its kind with notable members of the black community in their particular chosen fields. The talks took place before an audience, with the full collection of talks and subsequent audience conversations to be found in *Building Britannia: Life Experience With Britain*, published by New Beacon Books, the first Caribbean publishing house in the UK and founded by John.

Toynbee Hall: Established in 1884 in the East End of London and is a volunteer led organisation whose aim is to help individuals and communities find solutions to their problems and enable them, through specific projects, to fulfill their potential.

Jo [Joseph] Grimond: politician and leader of the British Liberal Party from 1956–1967.

[John] Enoch Powell: Conservative politician, sacked from the shadow cabinet for a speech made at a Conservative meeting in Birmingham in 1968, now commonly referred to as the 'Rivers of Blood' speech. In it, he quoted one of his constituents as saying to him: 'In 15–20 years' time the black man will have the whip hand over the white man.' Powell went on to say in his speech, 'How dare I say such a horrible thing…I do not have the right not to do so.' He continued by calling for imposed limits on immigration and 'the encouragement of re-emigration'. In his concluding warning about continued immigration he quoted Sybil in Virgil's Aeneid: 'As I look ahead, I am filled with foreboding; like the Roman, I seem to see "the River Tiber foaming with much blood".'

Pansy Jeffreys: Guyanese born social worker based in West London and founding member of the Berbice Housing Association.

Lee Samuel: Founder chairman of the Carib Housing Association, which built sheltered accommodation for elderly Caribbean people in London.

Confait Case: Maxwell Confait, a homosexual double ethnic man murdered in Catford, South London in 1972. The subsequent miscarriage of justice of the two youths convicted of his murder was one of the issues that brought about the Royal Commission on Criminal Procedure which recommended among other things the establishment of the Crown Prosecution Service and also led to the Police and Criminal Evidence Act 1984.

Sir Kenneth Newman: Commissioner of the Metropolitan Police from 1982–1987. Prior to this he was Chief Constable of the Royal Ulster Constabulary in Northern Ireland from 1976–1979.

Stephen Lawrence murder enquiry report [1999]: Chaired by High Court judge Sir William MacPherson and a panel of three advisors, including the Rt Revd Dr John Sentamu, then Bishop of Stepney. The report concluded that 'institutional racism' was prevalent within the Metropolitan Police and made 70 recommendations relating to the Police and other public bodies to tackle this issue.

Stephen Lawrence was an 18 year old student, stabbed and murdered by a racist gang in Eltham, South East London in 1993. No one has been convicted for his murder.

Herman Ouseley: Chair and Chief Executive of the Commission for Racial Equality from 1993–2000. He became a life peer, Baron Ouseley of Peckham Rye, in 2001.

Bill Morris: Jamaican born General Secretary of the Transport and General Workers' Union from 1991–2003. He became a life peer, Baron Morris of Handsworth, in 2006.

3. Decade of Evangelism

Rolan Adams: 15 year old who was stabbed and murdered by racist youths in the South East London in 1991, less than two miles away from where the murder of Stephen Lawrence took place later that year.

Ruhullah Aramesh: 24 year old Afghan refugee attacked and murdered by a racist gang in Thornton Heath, South London in 1992.

6. Japheth 'Jeff' Crawford of Barbados

Ralph Straker: Barbados born former employee at the Southwark Diocese Race Relations Commission. Awarded the Barbados Service Medal in 1980 and the OBE in 2002 for his service to the Caribbean community in London.

CXC certificate: secondary school examinations certificate issued by the Caribbean Examinations Council.

SECTION TWO: CALLED TO SERVE

11. The Rev'd Guy Hewitt Presiding at the Eucharist for the First Time
Rev'd Sandra and Rev'd Davidson Bowen: ordained deacons at the same time as Rev'd Guy Hewitt.

12. Tribute to David Udo on his retirement
Olive Morris [1952-979]: Jamaican born civil rights activist, community leader, Black Panther and founder of the Brixton Black Women's Group.

New Cross Massacre Campaign: Thirteen young people were killed in a house fire while attending a birthday party in New Cross, South East London in January 1981. The Police were initially unable to establish a cause of the fire, though many believe the teenagers were victims of an arson attack. No one has been convicted.

21. Bishop of Southwark's Staff Meeting
Last of the Summer Wine: Long running BBC television whimsical comedy, following the misadventures of three elderly friends in the autumn of their lives in the Yorkshire countryside

SECTION THREE: CHRIST IN CHURCH & SOCIETY

34. Accountability
Janani Luwum [1922 – 1977]
Archbishop of Uganda, Rwanda, Burundi and Boga-Zaire, murdered by Idi Amin's regime in 1977. His statue is one of ten commemorated Twentieth Century Martyrs to be found in the niches above the West Entrance of London's Westminster Abbey.

39. 'To educate or train – that is the question'
The Society of Headmasters and Headmistresses of Independent Schools is an Association of some 100 well established independent [fee paying] schools in the United

Kingdom. These include Bedales, Royal Russell School, King Edward VI High School for Girls, Royal Ballet School, Yehudi Menuhin School.

Further reading of this argument can be found in the Paper on Race Awareness Training given to Committee on Black Anglican Concerns on 7 December 1992, printed in Wilfred Wood's earlier book, *'Keep The Faith, Baby!'*, published by The Bible Reading Fellowship, 1994.